LOWER FAIRFOREST BAPTIST CHURCH

Union County, South Carolina

MINUTES 1809–1875

MEMBERSHIP LISTS THROUGH 1906

Transcribed and Edited by

Brent H. Holcomb

SCMAR
1997

HERITAGE BOOKS
2021

HERITAGE BOOKS

AN IMPRINT OF HERITAGE BOOKS, INC.

Books, CDs, and more—Worldwide

For our listing of thousands of titles see our website
at
www.HeritageBooks.com

Published 2021 by
HERITAGE BOOKS, INC.
Publishing Division
5810 Ruatan Street
Berwyn Heights, Md. 20740

International Standard Book Numbers
Paperbound: 978-0-7884-0663-8

INTRODUCTION

The name of the writer's ancestor, Benjamin Holcombe, has been indelibly written in the history of the Fairforest Baptist Church and in the history of the Baptist Church in upper South Carolina by his gift of two acres of land for the Fairforest Meeting. This gift is mentioned in Morgan Edwards' manuscript, *Materials Toward a History of the Baptist Denomination in America*. Leah Townsend's *South Carolina Baptists 1670-1805* (1935) gives an account of the establishment of the Fairforest Meeting in the 1760s. Mrs. Vera S. Spears wrote and published *The Fairforest Story*, a history of the Lower Fairforest Baptist Church, in 1974. Therefore, a lengthy history of this church is not necessary here. The minutes begin with the entry of 20 August 1809, when the Lower Fairforest Baptist Church was established as an arm of Padgett's Creek Baptist Church, which had been established in 1784. Some families who had belonged to the Fairforest Meeting prior to the Revolution were members of the Padgett's Creek church and later of the Lower Fairforest Church.

I have included the church minutes 1809-1875 and membership lists from the earliest list to the year 1906. Even the list of 1906 includes later entries concerning deaths and dismissions of members. These minutes cover the usual matters of church membership and discipline. Some dates of death and are included within the membership lists. Occasionally, maiden names of married women are indicated. However, Baptist church minutes do not, as a rule, provide records of births, marriages, and deaths. The names of slave members, often noting the names of their owners, are interwoven in the records and are included in membership lists of the Lower Fairforest Baptist Church, providing valuable information for African-American history and genealogy. I hope that this compilation will be helpful to historians, genealogists, and descendants of members of this early Union County church.

My sincere thanks to my friends Jo White Linn and Mike Becknell for their help in editing and proofing this work.

Brent H. Holcomb
March 22, 1997

MINUTES OF LOWER FAIRFOREST BAPTIST CHURCH

August 20th 1809. The members of Padget Creek Church on the north side of Tiger River convend by permission of said church at the Fairforest Brick Meeting house as an arm of the above said church to transact Business and enrolled the names of those that were present.

Sept. 23, 1809. Said church in conference and nothing done.

October 21, 1809. In church met and received Negro Beck by Experience.

November 25, 1809. In church conference and received Polly Greer[?] by experience.

December 23, 1809. Nothing done.

January 27, 1810. In church met and read Articles of Faith.

February 24, 1810. In church conference the brothern were unamomous in becoming constituted and apointed Brother Joshua Greer, William White to lay it before the Padget Creek Church.

March 24, 1810. Agreed to call for ministerial help to be with us, on the Saturday before the fourth Sabbath in May in order to constitute this.

April 21, 1810. Appointed Brother Philip Holcomb Deacon. Also agreed that this church go by the name of Lower Fairforest

May 25, Friday. Prepared for a constitution.

Be it remembered that on the 26 of May 1810 we subscribe being duly and legally called by a body of people professing the Baptist religion, Standing on Gospel Order known hereafter by the name of Lower Fairforest-- Agreebly our call have duly examined Same People expressing their Faith, we have by Authority of Jesus Christ set them apart, and on the constitution and of the Bethel Association, giving and allowing the full and independent authority to act within herself, as church properly organized, with ful power of Gospel Discipline receive or Suspend agreebly to the Scripture Taking that for their only Rule of life and Practice praying that the great head of the church, Jesus Christ may bless them in all of their laudable endeavors to promote his cause on Earth. Thomas S. Greer, Thomas Ray, Jas. Cooper, Nathan Langston, David Golightly.

Also the same day ordained Brother Philip Holcomb & Set him apart to the office of a Deacon. Also Received Susanna Whitlock and Negro Jane Tom by Letter.

June 23, 1810. In conference agreed on the next session to contribute of our substance to defray the charges of the church.

1

July 21, 1810. In church conference me met and Received Thomas Whitlock, Sarah Boatman. Received a petition (verbal) from Fairforest Church whishing to help to assist them In some difficulty and appointed Brother Philip Holcomb, Joseph Little, W. White to attend them, Also appointed Brother J. W. Cooper as Treasurer for the church-- Agreed to minister of our substance in a quarter for the use of the church.

August 21 1810. In conference. Received Dianna Boatman by Experience, Hetty Torrance by Letter. Also called in question the Sixth Article of our faith with respect to Elders & We Nominate Brethen Robt White Sen., Jas W. Cooper to be Ey'd by the church.

September 22, 1810. In church Conference we met & Recv'd Absalom Walker and Susanna Walker his wife & Negro Judah by letter.

October 27, 1810. In church conference met and granted a letter of Recommendation to Daniel Turner to the New Hope Church.

November 24, 1810. In church conference met and recd. N. Holcomb Negro Peg by Letter.

December 22. 1810. Called in Question the matter of elders but laid over for want of the men.

January 26, 1811. Laid over the matter of Br. Little & appointed Brethren Philip Holcomb, William White, Robt. Bullington. Ben. Nix to endeavor to settle the matter & to make report to next meeting.

February 23. 1811. In church conference met and Committee report not settled & after Collecting the mind of the church We lay[?] on Br. Little to confess to the above Brethren that he gave just cause for them to be hurt. Received a petition from Padget Creek church requesting Ministerial assistance to assist in the ordination of Deacons- their request granted & apointed Brethren Joshua Greer, Philip Holcomb, William White to attend them.

March 23, 1811. In church conference met & the Brethren Viz. J. W. Cooper, P. Simmons profess to be satisfied with Br. Little which is the church Satisfaction.

April 27, 1811. In church conference met and Sister Negro, Judith being a church charge. Brother Negro Tom agree to take her one month for Sum of three dollars.

May 1811. In conference met -- nothing done.

June 1811. In church Conference met and nothing done.

MINUTES OF LOWER FAIRFOREST BAPTIST CHURCH

July 27, 1811. In conference met and Sister Susanah Whitelock came and confessed of getting overcome with passion -- but laid over-- Brother Joshua Greer-- came and acknowledged a fault of taking too much spirituous Liquor & ask forgiven & restor'd to his ministry.

August 24, 1811. In conference met and Sister Whitlock not complying with the request of the church request of the church we still lay it over for her to see her wrong--- Also, deligated Brother Philip Holcomb, Joshua Greer to represent us before the association.

September 21, 1811. In church conference met and Sister Whitlock complying with the church request & we restore her to full fellowship.

October 1811. In church conference met and nothing done.

November 1811. In church conference met and put down Br. Negroe Tom for exercising his gift. Also Received a petition from Tinker Creek Church having Br. Joshua Greer to attend them Monthly as their preacher. Their request granted.

December 21, 1811. In church conference met & Br. Jesse Holcomb confessed a fault it being overcome with passion & was forgiven. Br. Negroe Tom not given full Satisfaction, we defer it till next meeting & we injoin it on them to be reconciled.

January 1812. In church conference met and nothing done.

February 22, 1812. In church conference met and laid over the matter of Br. Negroe Tom.

March 26, 1812. In church conference met and Brother Tom gave satisfaction and was forgiven and the church gave his gift.

April, Saturday 1812. In church conference and nothing done.

May 12. In church conference met and received Elizabeth White by letter and Polly Mayfield and Clary Little, Isabel Tucker, by experience-- Appointed Br. James W. Cooper clerk to set Tunes.

June 27, 1812. In conference met and received Benj. Holcomb, Joanna Mayfield by Letter.

July 1812 In church conference met and received Dolph and Ann of Toms by Experience and Gibbs Anne Johnson's Doll and Polly Howard by Letter.

August 1812. In Church conference met and received Joseph Little's Cuffy by Experience and Bennett and Daniel Tucker by Letter and delegated Brethren Philip Holcomb, Joshua Greer to present us to the association.

September 1812. In church conference met and Received Sarah Rountree by letter-- Sarah Steen by Experience.

October 24. 1812. Agreed that the Church meet on Wednesday the 4th of November 1812 in order for reconcilling, a difficulty between Sister Mary Reader and some of the sisters.

Sunday November 1, 1812. Received McBeth Prince and Tom by Experience.

Wednesday 4th. Met agreeable to appoint. And found Sister Reeder Guilty of the Charge laid against her and gave her till next meeting to give Satisfaction, if not, Excluded.

December 26, 1812. In church conference met and restored Sister Mary Reeder to fellowship.

January 23, 1813. In church conference met and dismissed Sister Hetty Torrance by letter.

February 27, 1813. In church conference met and received Benson's Negroe Shadrack by experience.

November 22, Sunday 1812. Received by experience negroe Sally and George McBeth.

January 24, 1813. Sunday received by experience Peter, Boson, Cudjoe of McBeths and Rountree's Lewis.

March 1813. In conference met and nothing done.

April 24, 1813. In conference met and complaint entered against Br. Joshua Greer for a report of intoxication. Not settled. appoints Thursday week to strive to Settle the matter. Appointed Brother Joseph Tucker to request Brother Joseph Howard of Tinker Creek to be with us on that day.

Sunday 25. Received Lucy McBeth negroe and Cap[?]. Charles by experience.

June 26, 1813. In church conference met and agreed to wait with Br. Greer longer- Also petitioned the Padget Creek and Upper Fairforest Churches for ministerial supplies.

Sunday 27, 1813. Received McBeth's Paul and Nancey by experience.

July 24, 1813. In conference met and Br. Joshua Greer came forward and gave satisfaction.

Sunday August 1, 1813. Received Negroe Caty McBeth by Experience-- Also too Negroes Cuffy and Rhoder under the watch care of the church.

MINUTES OF LOWER FAIRFOREST BAPTIST CHURCH

August 21, 1813. In church conference met and received Clary (of Thomas Greer) by experience--Also delegated Brethren Philip Holcomb, William White to represent this body to the Bethel Association.

September 25, 1813. In church conference met nothing done.

October 23, 1813. In church conference met and gave Brother Joshua Greer his Ministerial Gift.

November 27, 1813. In church conference met. Br. Jesse Holcomb came forward and acknowledged a fault of being out of the way by being angry-- was forgiven.

December 25, 1813. In church conference met and Excluded Negroe Cuffy (McBeth) from Society.

January 22, 1814. In church Conference met and reviewed the Articles of Faith.

February 26, 1814. In church conference met and dismissed J. W. Cooper and Elizabeth his wife by Letter.

March 26, 1814. In church conference met and Nothing done.

April 23, 1814. Met in Conference and Nothing Done.

May 22, 1814. In church conference met and nothing done.

July 23, 1814. In conference met and appointed the fourth Sabbath in September a Sacrimental Occasion.

August 7, 1814. In Church Conference met and delegated Brethren Caleb Greer, William White to represent us to the Association.

September 23, 1814. In conference met and read and approved the letter to the Association.

October 22, 1814. In church conference met and apointed Br. Robert White Jr. Music Clerk.

November 26, 1814. In church conference met and nothing done.

December 1814. In church conference met and nothing done.

January 21, 1815. In church conference met and nothing done

February 1815. In church conference met and agreed to acquaint the Black Brethren of this body, that it is wrong and contrary to Gospel discipline to

5

trade or traffic on the Sabbath.

March 1815. In church conference met and entered into Bro. Joshua Greer case -- laid over.

May 27, 1815, In church conference met and received Sally Boatman (wife of Jesse) by experience-- also agreed to wait with Br. Joshua Greer. Appoint Br. Holcomb to cite a Black Member to the next meeting whom he has labored with for acting contrary to church discipline.

June 24, 1815. In church conference met the Black Member Cuffy cited by Br. Holcomb came and gave satisfaction-- The case of Br. J. Greer by his request still defer'd.

July 1815. In church conference met and Excluded Br. Joshua Greer from fellowship. The next day received Negroe Hercuby and wife Jane by Letter.

Augusʳ 16, 1815. In church conference met and delegated Brethren Philip Holcomb and William White and in case of failure Br. Caleb Greer to represent this body to the Association.

September 23, 1815. In conference met Dismissed Polly Rhodes, Bennett Tucker, and Isabel Tucker and Sarah Steen by Letter.

October 1815. In conference met nothing done.

November 24, 1815. In church conference met. A complaint entered against Brother Negro Cuffy for in practice contrary to Gospel order, appointed Br. Joseph Little to cite him to appear tomorrow before the church.

24th. Agreeable to appoint met and upon Br. Cuffy's promising to comply with the requisition of the church, the church agreed to wait with him.

December 1815. In conference met and nothing done.

January 1816. In church conference met and nothing done, nothing came before the church.

February 1816. In conference met and nothing done.

March 23, 1816. In conference met nothing done.

April 27, 1816. In church conference met and agreed that Br. Negro Tom be at Liberty to go or attend anywhere in the Adjacent District to Exercise his Gift of Singing, Prayer, and Exhortation.

MINUTES OF LOWER FAIRFOREST BAPTIST CHURCH

May 25, 1816. In church conference met and agreed that the members of this Body at the meeting after communion to render their reason for not Partaking of the Lords Supper.

June 22, 1816. In church conference met and agreed that Br. Caleb Greer purchase a Bible and Hymn Book for the use of the church.

July 1816. In conference met and nothing done.

August 24, 1816. Met in church conference and received Polly White by Experience-- Also delegated Brethren Philip Holcomb and William White to represent us before the Association.

September 26, 1816. In church conference met and nothing done.

October 26, 1816. In church conference met and Dismissed Benj. and Sarah Holcomb his wife by letter.

November 1816. Prevented by Wet Weather.

November 3, 1816. Sunday received by Experience Gist's Jack.

December 27, 1816. In church conference met and nothing done.

January 25, 1817. In church conference met and nothing done.

February, 25, 1817. In church conference met and nothing done.

March 1817. In church conference met and nothing done.

April 26, 1817. In church conference met and took up the case of Sister Whitlock leaving her husband, and after hearing from both parties, agreed that Sister Whitlock is chargeable -- and agreed that she be admonished and the church agreed to wait with her. A complaint against Sister Boatman entered, widow for living in disorder and appointed Brother Jesse Holcomb to cite her to attend the next meeting. Also a complaint entered against Brother Joseph Reader by Brother W. Izrel (member of Fairforest Church) for defrauding of him. Appointed Br. Philip Holcomb to cite him to attend the next meeting.

May 27, 1817. In church conference met and took up the case of Brother Reeder and hearing from him, and submitting it to the church and settled it-- Also excluded Sarah Boatman for living in disorder.

June 27, 1817. Nothing done prevented by Harvest.

July 26, 1817. In church conference met and Brother Negroe Prince entered a complaint against Sister Negro Jane, herently [sic] his wife for not performing the duty of a wife toward her husband, Agreed that Br. Negroe Tom cite her to attend the first Sunday in next month to answer for herself.

Sunday. Agreeable to appointment, met and hearing from both parties agreed to retain them in fellowship. After an Admonition from us.

August 12, 1817. In church conference met and a complain entered against Brother Negro Cuffy for living in disorder-- appointed Br. Jesse Boatman to cite him to attend next meeting to answer for himself.

October 18, 1817. In church conference met and nothing done.

November 22, 1817. In church conference met and nothing done.

December 17, 1817. In church conference met and dismissed Negro Beck Simmons by letter. And excluded Negroe Cuffy for loos and unchristian conduct.

January 24, 1818. In church conference met and excluded Negroe Jane McBeth.

February 21, 1818. In church conference met and Brother Bennet Tucker and his wife Isabel who were dismissed some time back, not entered any other church, returned back to us and are considered as members of this body-- Also received Merium Cooper by experience.

March 1818. No meeting prevented by Court.

April 25, 1818. In church conference met and excluded Susanna Whitlock from the church.

May 24, 1818. In church conference met and received Br. Robert B. Hines by Experience.

June 27, 1818. In church conference met and excluded Br. Hayes Charles from this body for disorderly conduct.

July 1818. In church conference met and dismissed Sister Susanna Simmons by letter. Also received Catherine Bruton by experience.

August 22, 1818. In church conference met and received Isaac P. Murphy by experience--also received Thomas Cooper by experience and delegated Brethren Phillip Holcomb, William White to attend the Bethel Association the next day received George Bruton by experience.

September 26. 1818. In church conference met and received Negroe Phoebe (Hunt) Nancy Holcomb, Franky Holcomb, and Cassey Woodson by experience, and dismissed Joseph and Betty Little his wife by letter. The next day received Negroe Bet (Luke), Frank, Judah, and Jinny (Thompson) by experience.

October 24, 1818. In church conference met and received Edith Jackson, Polly Jackson, Elizabeth Holcomb, Patty Mulky by experience. The next day received Negroe Anthony (Mary Means) by experience.

November 21, 1818. In church conference met and received James P. Woodson, Susanna Mulkey by experience. A complaint entered against Lewis Roundtree for disorderly conduct and appointed Brethren Joseph Reeder, Negroe Tom to cite him to attend next meeting-- Also dismissed Brother Robert White and his wife Poly by letter-- Also appointed Br. George Bruton as Music Clerk in this church.

December 24, 1818. In church conference met and received John Mayfield, Barth Mayfield, Nancy Nix, Dolly Tucker, and William David's negroe Ben by experience.

January Sunday the 24th 1819. received Negroes Agness Clowney and negro William Gremky by experience.

February 27, 1819. In church conference met and nothing done.

March 27, 1819. In church conference met and Sister Dicey Bullington under the watch care-- the next day (Sunday) received Ruth Thompson's negroe Paul by experience.

April 24, 1819. In church conference met and received Benj. and Salley Holcomb and the Rev. L. Charles Therber by letter.

May 22, 1819. In church conference appointed Brethren Philip Holcomb, William White, Thomas Cooper, George Bruton, Jesse Holcomb to look into the difficulty or piece of conduct alleged to Negroe Ben belonging to William Davitt, Esq. and make report to next meeting -- also took Brother Hezekiah McDougal under the care of the church.

June 1819. Met in church conference and nothing done.

July 24, 1819. In church conference met and excluded William Davitt's negroe Ben for talking disorderly. Also received negroe Phillip (Goodwin) by experience--The next day received Daniel Palmer's negroe wench Nelly by experience.

August 21, 1819 In church conference met and delegated Brother Caleb Greer, William White to represent this body to the Bethel Association.

September 25, 1819 In church conference met and received Betty Farmer by experience also received a petition from Brother Paton Simmons requesting a rehearing--the request granted.

October 23, 1819. In church conference met and received Levina Greer, Elizabeth Hart, by experience--And Sunday received negroe Matilda (John White's) by experience.

November 27, 1819. In church conference met and received Polly Gregory, Nancy Woodson by experience, also dismissed Brother Paton Simmons by letter.

December 1819. In church conference met and nothing done.

January 22, 1820. In church conference met and nothing done--on the next day Sunday dismissed Negroe Frank (John White) by letter.

February 26, 1820. In church conference met and nothing done.

March 25, 1820. In church conference met and agreed unanimously that Brother Thomas Cooper be chosen as deacon to supply the place of Brother Phillip Holcomb, deceased.

April 1820. In church conference met and appointed William White to cite Br. negroe Tom to attend next meeting to render his reason for non attendance at church meetings.

May 27, 1820. In church conference met and received Br. John Powell by letter-- also brother Negroe Tom came forward and rendered his reason for non attendance, also acknowledged a fault of retailing spirits and was forgiven. Agreed that at the next meeting take into consideration the Gift of Brother negroe Tom. Received Murphy's negroe Beack by experience.

June 24, 1820. In church conference met, and licensed Br. Negroe Tom to improve his talents where God in his providence may call him. Also excluded Br. James P. Woodson for disorderly conduct and inattentiveness to attend church meeting.

A complaint entered against Br. George Bruton for immorality and appointed Br. L. C. Thurber to cite him to attend next meeting. On Sunday the 25th received Lucinda Lee and Negroe Charles (Bates) by Experience.

July 1820 received Gerimah Lee by letter.

July 22. In church conference met and received Priscilla Gibbs, John Murrell by Experience and the case of Br. Bruton laid over.

MINUTES OF LOWER FAIRFOREST BAPTIST CHURCH

August 26, 1820. In church conference met and Br. George Bruton came forward confessed his fault and was forgiven-- Also received negroe Minna (Duncan) and Nancy Bullinton by Experience.

September 23. In church conference met and nothing done.

October 21, 1820. In church conference met and dismissed Brother negroe Paul (Thompson) and negroe Jinny (Thomson) by letter.

November 25. In church conference met and agreed that Br. John Powel have a letter of dismission when call'd for. Dismissed Br. John Powel by Letter.

December 1820. In church conference met and a committee appointed to look into the standing of Brother Negroe Tom, and the committee report that Brother Tom did not exercise his public gift until satisfaction is made by Br. Tom.

December 25. Received James Mitchell's negroe Deal by Experience.

January 27, 1821. In church conference met and received Mr. Duncan's negroe Delf by experience-- also Brother Negroe Tom come forward and gave satisfaction and the church set him at liberty and give him his gift.

February 24, 1821. In church conference met and nothing done.

March 24, 1821. In church conference met and excluded Brother George Bruton for immorality and non attendance. Also called in question a difficulty Sister Frances Holcomb involved hereafter by entering a suit in law without leave of the church, and also by entertaining a spirit of malice and revenge.

April 21, 1821. In church conference met and took into consideration of the circumstances of Sister Frances Holcomb and agreed to Lay it over in order to convince her of her error.

May 26, 1821. In church conference met and excluded Frances Holcomb from the fellowship of this church.

June 1821. In church conference met and nothing done.

July 21, 1821. In church conference met and received Thomas Hart Sr. by experience.

August 25. 1821. In church conference met and took up the case of Brother Jesse Holcomb in that we judge he hath been exercised by a hard and malicious spirit, agreed to lay it over.

September 1821. In church conference met and a complaint entered by Br. Caleb Greer against Sister Betsy Malone for accusing him of malpractice in the execution of his office, no satisfaction laid over Delegated Brethren L. C. Thurber and Thomas Cooper to attend the association.

October 1821. In church conference met and charge against Br. Daniel Tucker for a beating and abusing his wife --he not being present laid it over.

November and December. Wet and no meeting.

January 26, 1822. Met in church conference and labor'd with Sister Betsy Malone, agreed to lay it over till next meeting.

February 23, 1822. In church conference met and Excluded Sister Betsy Malone.

March 23, 1822. In church meeting met and ordained Br. Thomas Cooper and set him apart to the office of Deacon.

April 1822. Wet and no meeting.

May 25, 1822. In church meeting met and excluded Brother Daniel Tucker for disorderly conduct.

July 27, 1822. In church conference met and dismissed Bro. Negroe Hercules to join some other church more convenient.

August 24, 1822. In church conference met and delegated Brethren Thomas Cooper, William White to attend the association.

First Sunday in August 1822. Received negroe Phoebe (Wallace) by experience. but conduct proving bad excluded.

September 21, 1822. In church conference met and dismissed Sister Dolly Tucker to join another church now [sic] convenient.

October 1822. In church conference met and received, negroe Mingoe by letter--also brother negroe Tom made his complaint to the church that in his opinion there is a majority (from the lack of ordained ministers) to set him apart to administer ordinance. postponed til next meeting for consideration.

November 23, 1822. In church conference met and took into consideration of setting Brother Tom apart to administer ordinances but acceded to or approv's of, but agreed that Br. Tom lay down his gift till the church be satisfied with him.

December 21, 1822. In church conference met and dismissed Sister Nancy Barnett.

MINUTES OF LOWER FAIRFOREST BAPTIST CHURCH

The first Sunday in December Brother negroe Tom gave the church satisfaction.

January 25, 1823. In church conference met and nothing done.

February 22, 1823. In church conference met and dismissed Sister Polly Harris and Edith Murphy to join another church more convenient. Also as there is some unfavorable report against Br. Tom agreed that Br. Tom lay down his gift till they are cleared up.

March 22, 1823. In church conference met and dismissed Sister Nancy Jackson by letter-- Also took up the case of Br. Tom and his wife-- laid over. Also Sister negroe Ester (Jackson) being cramped being in the church, and also being guilty of immoral conduct and wishing to be excluded, and no promise of amendement, agreed to exclude her from the privilege of the church. Agreed to convene on the fourth Sabbath in May next.

Sunday 3 May 1829. In church conference met and excluded negroe Cato from society.

Saturday 23 May 1829. In church conference met and dismissed Robert White Sr. and his wife Elizabeth by letter-- by the absence of Br. Thomas Willard from meeting agreed that William Gregory request him to attend the next meeting-- also appointed William White to attend us at our next meeting to answer to some reports circulating against him.

Saturday June 27, 1829. In church conference met and received Sister Nancy Woodson by letter-- Brother Gregory reported that he cited Brother Willard, and he not being present agreed that we lay it over till next meeting-- Brother Anderson appeared and gave General Satisfaction.

Sunday 28. Brother George Kershaw and Wife Elizabeth was received under the watch care of the church.

July 25, 1829. In church conference met and received Elizabeth Woodson, Sr. and Elizabeth Woodson Jr. by letter, Brother Willard attended and acknowledged that he is careless in attending church meeting, but submitted himself to the church-- the church admonished him to be more attentive to his future attendance.

August 22, 1829. In church conference met and entered into a resolution to have the business or minutes of the preceeding meeting read-- A motion made by Br. Kershaw that we enrol the names of all the male members of this body that are present every conference, the motion put to a vote, and lost, and agreed to put it to vote the next meeting. A motion made by Br. Kershaw to have the business of the church in private conference to be put to vote next meeting. A motion made by Br. E. Greer to have the sums contributed by the members to the church for the use of the church be annex'd to their names. Delegated Brethren Elijah Greer and William Gregory and in case of failure, Brother Caleb Greer to represent us at the Bethel Association. John Harlan restored to fellowship.

September 26, 1829. In church conference met put the motion whether every male member should be minuted every conference--lost. The motion to have the business of the church in private put to a vote--lost. Motion to have the sums contributed annex'd to their names--put to a vote and carried. Br. Benjamin Holcomb entered a complaint against Br. B. B. Pines for imbibing poison tenets and living an idle and disorderly life and every one to inform him of his accusation and request him to attend. Sister Nancy Woodson and Cassey Perkins applied for letters of dismission in case they should move before next meeting-- agreed that they should call on the clerk, if need require for letter. Letter of dismission was given them about the 15 of October dated from this time.

October 24, 1829. In church conference met and nothing done.

November 21, 1829. In church conference met and excluded Br. Hines. By the absence of Sister Telitha Jackson from appointed Br. N. Holcomb and Br. B. Holcomb to request her to attend our next meeting.

December 26, 1829. In church conference met and took up the case of Sister Jackson--her not being present--laid over until next meeting.

January 23, 1830. In church conference met and excluded Sister Jackson from Society for living a disorderly life and using bad language. Also excluded Br. Luke Bailey from society for purloining. Appointed Brother Elijah Greer to act as clerk for the church.

February 27, 1830. Met in church conference nothing done.

March 27, 1830. Met in church conference and by the absence of Br. Charles Bates negro and some unfavorable reports appointed Brethren Thomas S. Greer, Caleb Greer and William Gregory to attend out next meeting.

April 24, 1830. Met in church conference --received Johnson Coggin and his wife by experience-- took up the case of Br. Charles Bates laid over till the first Sunday in May.

May 1, 1830. Sunday met and excluded Charles Bates.

May 22. Met in church conference and received Samuel White and Sarah White by experience.

First Sunday in June. Met and tolerated Br. Frank to sing and pray and exort.

June 23, Met in church conference--entered a charge against Br. John Harlan -- laid over till first Sabbath in July.

First Sabbath in July. Took up the case of Br. John--laid over until next meeting in coarse. Also charges brought to light against Sister Edith Harlan. Excluded for living disorderly life.

July 24, 1830. Met in church conference and took up the case of Sister Patsy Brewton for living disorderly life--Excluded.

August 21. Met in church conference and took up the case of Br. John Harlan and excluded him from society. Also delegated Brethren E. Greer, Samuel White and in case of failure to represent us to the association Br. C. Greer. Also appointed E. Greer to prepare a letter for the association.

September 25. Met in church conference. Read the letter for the association and made a collection.

October 25. Met in church conference and excluded Harlan's Caroline for disorderly conduct. Granted letters to Sister Elizabeth and Sarah White.

First Sunday in November. Met and in church conference a charge brought to lite against Br. George Brewton for intemperance and excluded. Also granted letters to Sisters Catharine Brewton, Sister Lucy Putmen.

November 27. Met in church conference and received Br. George Kershaw and his wife Elizabeth by letter. By the absence of Brethren John Anderson and Thomas Willard from meeting agreed that Br. Gregory and Br. Kershaw cite them to attend out next meeting.

December 25, 1830. Met in church conference Br. Anderson gave satisfaction Br. Willard not being present laid over until next meeting.

January 22, 1831. Met in church conference and dismissed Br. Samuel White.

February 25, 1831. Met in church conference and renewed the citation of Br. Willard by his being absent.

March 25, 1831. Met in church conference and nothing done.

April 23, 1831. Met in church conference and took up the case of Bro. Willard and excluded him from society. Received Amus McBeth by experience.

May 21. Met in church conference and by the absence of Bro. Anderson from meeting agreed that Brethren Gregory and Caleb Greer cite him to attend our next meeting.

June 25. Met in church conference and took up the case of Br. Anderson and laid over until our next meeting, and dismissed Br. Joe Gibbs by letter.

July 23. Met in church conference and took up the case of Br. Anderson laid over until next meeting and by and by the absence of Basset Woodson from meeting agreed that Br. Aaron Harland cite him to attend the first Sunday in August.

August 27, 1831. Met in church conference and took up the case of Br. John Anderson and excluded him --laid over Br. Bassett's case until the first Sunday in September--delegated Brethren William Gregory, Elijah Greer and Caleb Greer in case of failure to Represent us to the association. Br. C. Greer to prepare a letter for the some.

September First Sunday. Br. Basset gave satisfaction.

September 25, 1831. Met in church conference and read the association letter and approved.

October 1831. Met in church conference and received Br, Joe Gibbs by letter.

April 21, 1832. Met in church conference and appointed Br. Isaac P. Murphy clerk.

June 23, 1832. Met in church conference granted Br. George Kershaw and wife a letter of dismission. Also received Mary Robinson by experience. Also granted out beloved sister Charlotte Murphy a letter of dismission.

July 21, 1832. Met in church conference and excluded Br. Charles Therber. Martha Greer joined by experience. Received Mary Carrol she having been baptized before. Received Holly Sparks by experience. Concluded to have our eyes on Br. Benjamin Holcomb as a person to fill the office of deacon.

July 22. Lord's day received Nancy Murell by experience.

August 25th 1832. Met In church conference and received the following persons by experience--Mitchel O. Sparks, John Gibbs, Sarah Greer, Russia White, Nelly Gibbs, Anna White, Elias White, Priscilla Browning.

September 21st. Met in church conference and delegated Brethren Holcombe and Wm Gregory to represent in the Association.

September 23, 1832. Met and received by experience the following persons Sally White, widow, Sally White, John P. Woodson, James Woodson, and Nancy his wife, James Woodson's Mitchel. Robert Woodson called the case of appointing deacon and laid over till next meeting.

September 24. Lord's Day received James Woodson son of Robert Woodson by experience.

October 9, 1832. Set in Capacity to receive members and received Churchel Gibbs and his wife Sarah, Thomas Woodson, James Hay, Avry Little, Clemmens Howard, and Anna Greer.

October 27, 1832. Met in church conference and received by experience Nancy Gregory, Robert Browning, Sr., Polly Hay, Jason Greer, Monroe Robertson. Appointed Brother Benjamin Holcomb to the office of Deacon and to be ordained on the Friday before the 4th Lord's Day in November next.

October 28, 1832. Lord's Day received by experience Susan Woodson, Julia Harlan, John Tate, Polly Tucker.

November 23, 1832. In church conference met and received a letter from the Sharon Baptist Church, Georgia, Henry County, stating their satisfaction with Br. James P. Woodson whom we had excomunicated and requesting a letter of dismission for him. Upon their statement we restored him and granted him a letter.

November 24, 1832. In church conference met and received by experience James Roberts, granted a letter to Sister Nancy Browning.

December 22, 1832. Met in church conference and received by experience Susan Greer. Laid over the ordination of Deacon Until next meeting.

December 23, 1832. Lord's Day met and received by experience Caleb Greer's Dicey, Thomas Greer's Willis and Widow Dicey Holcomb.

December 25. Met and restored Sister Ede (Aaron Harlan's).

January 26, 1833. Met in church conference and granted Sister Nancy White a letter of dismission. Laid over the ordination of Deacon until the meeting in February next send petition to our sister churches the Upper Fairforest and Padget's Creek for help.

February 23, 1833. Met in church conference. Received Susan Gibbs by letter. Received help from Padgett's Creek and set apart Brother Benjamin Holcomb to the office of Deacon.

February 24, 1833. Lord's Day received by experience Bob (Sister Reader's) and Sally (Bird Murphy).

March 3, 1833. Met in church conference and granted letters of dismission to Brother James Roberts. Received by experience Robert Boatman.

April 27, 1833. Met in church conference and received the letter of dismission which we granted to Brother George Kershaw and wife in June last.

May 25, 1833. Met in church conference nothing done.

June 22, 1833. Met in church conference and received a letter from Brother James P. Woodson requesting a recommendation and likewise a letter of dismission. We agree to answer his letter, but not to give him a letter of dismission having done it before.

July 27, 1833. Met in conference and received a letter from Brother J. Davis of Fairforest requesting conference in a camp meeting, but we cannot comply-- Likewise a petition from Padgett Creek for help and granted help via Caleb Greer, William Gregory, B. Holcomb, and John Gibbs.

August 24, 1833. Met in church conference and received a letter from the Woodward Baptist Church respecting Brother G. Kershaw which we agree to answer. Also appointed Brother B. Holcomb and William Gregory delegates to the next association. Brother Caleb Greer in case of failure and Brother Jason Greer to write the association letter.

September 21, 1833. Met in conference and read the association letter, Heard the experience of Sister Holcomb's Tony and approved it but there was some objection to his being received on account of a difficulty between him and one of our members.

October 26, 1833. Met in church conference and dismissed Susan Anderson by letter.

January 25, 1834. Met in conference and granted letters of dismission to Brother James Woodson and wife Nancy Woodson, to his negro man Mitchel, Thomas Woodson's Jane, also to Sister Russia Wilbanks-- formerly Russia White. Likewise nominated Brethren William Gregory, John White, and Elias White to visit Sister Susan Holcomb respecting a difficulty between herself and Sister Dicey Holcomb's Tony. Nominated Brethren J. Greer, J. Hay, J. Gibbs, C. Greer. and B. Holcomb a committee to attend to the repairing our seats and building galleries.

February 22, 1834. Met in conference and dismissed sister Nelly Norman formerly Nellie Gibbs by letter. Heard the report of the committee appointed to visit Sister Susan Holcomb which being favorably received Sister Dicey Holcomb's Tony was a member with us.

March 22, 1834. Met in church conference and nothing done.

April 26, 1834. Met in conference and nominated Brother Jason Greer Clerk of the church to Supply the place of Brother Murphy. Received the acknowledge of Brother Charles Therber unanimously. Also nominated James Hay to site Billy (McBeth) for disorderly conduct.

May 24, 1836. No meeting in consequence of the weather.

June 1, 1834. First Sunday met in conference and took up the case of Billy (McBeth) and after a notice and investigation of his conduct-- Excluded him.

June 21, 1834. Met in conference and appointed Brother John P. Woodson to cite Brother Thomas Woodson to attend the church meeting to account for his nonattendance at church.

July 26, 1834. In conference met and received by experience Dicey Sanders, and Frances Davis. Agreeable to the reference of last meeting Brother Thomas Woodson came forward and proceded to make concession satisfactory to the church. Agreed to write Brother A. Little to know why he has not given the church, notice of his intentions of staying so long. Nominated Brother James Woodson to cite Brother Harlin to attend conference meeting to account for disorderly conduct.

August 3, 1834. First Sunday met in conference and took up the case of brother Aron Harlin and concluded to lay it over till next meeting.

August 23, 1834. In conference met Proceeded to receive by experience Eleanor Bishop and also Sarah Tate by letter. Took up the case of Brother Harlin and after an investigation to his conduct excluded him. Appointed Brother James Hay to cite Sister Polly (Holcomb) to attend our next meeting to answer charges which is alledged her. Delegated our Brothers William Gregory, Benjamin Holcomb and in case of failure Jason Greer to represent us in the next association. Also appointed Brother Jason Greer to write the association letter.

September 7, 1834. Sunday, Met In conference and received by experience Prince (Prewit). Took up the cause of Sister Polly (Holcomb) and concluded to lay it over till the next meeting-- then bring proof to sustain the charges against her.

September 27, 1834. In conference met and dismissed by letter Brother John Tate and Sarah Tate his wife. Read and approved the association letter.

October 25, 1834. In conference met. First--received by experience Spencer Greer. Second--Granted letters of dismission to Sister Sarah Holcomb and Charlotte Harlin. Third--Took up a letter from Flat Creek Church, Ga., Hall County, concerning Sister Elizabeth Malone in which they gave a clean account of her and stated that they had fellowship with her, and requested us to restore her and give her a letter of dismission which request the church granted. Fourth--Appointed Brother Jason Greer, Treasurer to fill the vacancy occasioned by the death of our beloved Brother Caleb Greer, decd. And also appointed the following Brothern, J. Hay, Spencer Greer, C. Thurber, W. Gregory, and B. Holcomb a committee to examine into the affairs of treasury and turn over to the present Treasurer.

October 26, 1834. In conference met and dismissed our Sister Julia (Harlin) Melton.

November 22, 1834. Met in conference and agreeable to the reference of last meeting; the committee appointed to examine into the affairs of the church fund Book--made a report and find $2.43 3/4 cash on hand and .68 3/4 due the church. The committee on improvement give back the business of the church without report and appointed the following Brethren viz: William Gregory, Benjamin Holcomb, and Jason Greer a committee to superintend the same business.

December 27, 1834. In conference met and received the report of the committee on improvement. Brother James Hay returned the deed of land on which this church and the church consigned them to the care of the Treasurer. Took in consideration the making of a new pulpit and for that purpose appointed Brother Benj. Holcomb and Elias White to do the work after their own form.

January 24, 1835. In conference met and nothing done.

February. Met in conference and nothing done.

March 21, 1835. in conference met and received the account of Brother Holcomb and White for building a pulpit which was $15.00.

April 25, 1835. In Conference met and received by letter Betsy Ann Bobo and also set a part the fourth Sunday in June for Communion.

May 25, 1835. In conference met and excluded from Baptism a colored man named Prince for his disorderly conduct and previous experience.

June 7, 1835. In conference met and received by experience Jim Murphy.

June 27, 1835. In conference met. First--Postponed the communion till the 4th Sunday in July the meeting to commence Friday before for the purpose of transacting business of the church. Second--Excluded negro Dicey (Greer). Also appointed Brother John P. Woodson to cite Sister Polly Willard to attend our next conference meeting to answer to complaint of an unfavorable report. Third-- Took into consideration the making of two windows in gable end of meeting house and for the purpose set apart the Thursday and Friday before the third Sunday in July for the Brethren to meet and do said work. Fourth-- Took into consideration the inexpediency of the Black people going into the

Galleries and concluded not to suffer them to go therein without a special invitation by motion of Brother J. Greer. Fifth--Took into consideration the expediency of having our practical rules of discipline drafted and for the purpose appointed the following Brethren a committee to draw up said rules (i. e) Brethren John Gibbs, Jason Greer, Mitchel Sparks and William Gregory. To report at the next meeting. Sixth--Collected the sum of five dollars and 97 cents.

July 5, 1835. In conference met and received by experience Negro Enoch Wilburn.

July 25, 1835. In conference met and first heard the report of Bro. John P. Woodson concerning Sister Polly Willard which was unfavorable and after an investigation of her conduct, excluded her from fellowship. Heard the report of the Committee on rules and concluded to defer it till tomorrow.

Saturday 25. In conference met. First--Received the report of the committee on rules of discipline which are drafted on Page 3. Second--Appointed a committee of the following Brethern-- W. Gregory, B. Holcomb, J. Hay, J. Gibbs, and J. Greer to arrange the preaching for the morrow. Third--Brother Holcomb entered a complaint against Negro Barbry cause laid over till next meeting.

July 27, 1835, Monday 27th in conference met and received by experience Polly Greer. Tuesday 28th in conference met and received by experience Patsy Howard.

August 22, 1835. In conference met and received by experience Sam (Wallace) and Jeffrey (Sparks). Also restored Charles Bates and Jessy (Duncan).

August 22, 1835. In conference met and First-- received by experience Deliah Boatman, Lina Jackson, Teletha Presley, Elizabeth Sparks, Nancy Asbiller Greer, Jesse Greer, and Polly Estes.

Second--Received by letter James C. Kitchens. Third-- Delegated Brethren Jason Greer, William Gregory, and in case of failure Brother John Gibbs to represent us in the next association. Also appointed Brother Jason Greer to write the Association letter to be read at our next meeting and also constituted the sum of $1.50 for the printing of the minutes. Also called the case of Brother B Holcomb against Sister Negro Barbry and concluded to suspend it till the first Sunday.

August 30, 1835. In conference met and dismissed our Brother and Sister Negroes Lawson and Tillie his wife. Received by experience Mary Gibbs, Lydia Kitchens and negro Abram (Palmers).

September 6, 1835. First Sunday in conference met. 1st-- Received by experience Negro Henry and Negro James (Wilborn) and negro Ben

(Holcomb) being long since baptized by Rev. J. Booker. 2nd-- Restored Sister Negro Nina (Rice). 4th--Took under consideration the gift of Brother Anthony and after a certain consideration of the matter concluded that he exercise no further than to exhort to sing & pray. 5--Took up the cause of Brother Holcomb against Sister Negro Barbary and referred to a committee of the following Brethern (i. e.) W. Gregory, J. Greer, C. Howard, J. C. Kitchens, E. White, M. Sparks, and Jesse Greer. Who succeeded in settling the matter satisfactory to both parties. 6th-- collected the sum of $1.12½ from the Black people.

September 26, 1835. In conference met. First--received by experience Mary Gibbs and Jane Rogers. Second--Read and approved the association letter. Third--Contributed to Rev. T. S. Greer $5.00 for defraying his expenses to the association and also gave our delegates W. Gregory and J. Greer $1.50 each-- $3.00. Fourth--On motion suspended the first Sunday meeting till the church see fit to order it again. Fifth--Collected the sum of $,3.25.

September 27, 1835. In conference met and received by experience Negro Caty (Gist).

October 25, 1835. In conference met. First--received by experience Susannah Holcomb. Also granted letters of dismission to Brother Holcomb and wife and daughter Susan. Second--Agreed that the clerk be authorized to make a settlement with Brother Holcomb and to pay him what is due him by this church. Third-- Called the case of Billy McBeth and postponed the same till next meeting.

November 21, 1835. In conference met. First received by letter Brother Tate and Wife. Second--Took up the cause of Billy (McBeth) and concluded to suspend any further discussion on the matter unless Billy came forward and make confession satisfactory to the church. Third--Agreed to sell lot of surplus brick at auction-- which was done by the clerk and went at the rate of 40 cents per hundred.

December 26, 1835. In conference met and took in consideration the granting of Brother J. P. Woodson a letter of dismission, but there being objection--the matter was suspended till next meeting. Second--Appointed a committee of the following Brethren J. C. Kitchen, M. Sparks, E. White, J. Gibbs and I. P. Murphy to look into the affairs of an old subscription. Third--Collected the sum of eight dollars and 18 3/4 cents. Fourth--Received the report of the committee with general satisfaction.

December 27, 1835. In conference met and received Negro Mariah (Fincher), also dismissed Brother George Kershaw and wife Elizabeth.

January 23, 1836. In conference met and took up the cause of Brother John P. Woodson and after reconsidering the same concluded to grant him and wife a letter. Collected the sum of $1.25.

MINUTES OF LOWER FAIRFOREST BAPTIST CHURCH

February 27, 1836. In conference met. First--Dismissed Brother John Tate and Sarah, his wife, also dismissed Sister Mary Gibbs. Second---Received Sister Sarah Stone by letter.

March 26, 1836. In conference met. First-- Dismissed Sister Sarah Stone also received Brother Henry Garrett and Elizabeth his wife by letter. Second--in addition to the nomination of Brethren J. W. Hay and John Gibbs to the office of deacon the church nominated Brethren Elias White, Mitchell Sparks, and Munroe Robinson and Henry Garrett also concluded to converse freely with the above named persons on the subject above suggested and out of the number to select one (by the Assistance of our Redeemer) to be set apart to the office of Deacon. Third--Suspended our collection till the next meeting. Fourth-Set apart the 4th Sunday in May for a communion Service.

April 23, 1836. In conference met and dismissed Sister Betsy Ann Bobo also received Brother Hyram Murphy and Elizabeth his wife by letter. Second Put off the appointment of a Deacon till out next meeting also put off the communion season till the 4th Sunday in June. Third--Collected the sum of $2.92 cents and concluded to have a First Sunday meeting in June for the purpose of seeing the Black members of our church. Fourth--Appointed a committee of the following brethren (i.e.) J. Greer, J. Gibbs, H. Garrett, E. White and Hyram Murphy to examine into the expediency of having a Rock blown or blasted which overhangs and obstrucks the Spring-- and to report at next meeting. Fifth--heard an acknowledgment of Brother J. C. Kitchens in which he States that he has been far out of the way therefore, craves the prayers of the church. The church appointed a committee of Brethren H. Garrett, J. Gibbs, W. Gregory, Jesse Holcomb, J. Hay and Hyram Murphy to inquire into the case of Brethren Kitchens and report at next meeting.

May 21, 1836. In conference met and postponed all the principle business of the church till the next meeting in consequence of many of the Brethren being called away on military duty. Second-- received a letter from Rev. Sterling Roberts of Georgia, Gwinnett County--with the request to give information respecting Brother James P. Woodson--Request granted.

June 25, 1836. In conference met. First--Received the report of the committee but suspended the entire passage of the sale till next meeting. Second--Nominated Brother Henry Garrett to the office of Deacon to fill the place of Brother Holcomb removed. Third--appointed a meeting to commence at this place the Friday before the 4th Sunday in August for the purpose of ordaining a Deacon, holding a communion Season etc. which meeting will be protracted if circumstances will justify the project.

July 3, 1836. In conference met Appointed a meeting the first Sunday in August to hear Anthony (Means) preach and to judge of his gift.

July 23, 1836. In conference met. First Dismissed Sister Frances Davis. Second--Took up the matter of the committee referred to at the last Meeting.

Brother Kitchens came forward and consented or agreed to the report (which is here drafted)

Report of the Committee

We the undernamed Brethren and Committee appointed by this church to examine into the case of Brother Thomas C. Kitchens, after a serious contemplation and hope, prayerful examination, whereas he cannot be retained in this church agreeable to Gospil discipline therefore distressing as it is to our feeling we think our duty to declare a nonfellowship, June 25, 1836.
William Gregory
Henry Garrett
John Gibbs
Hyram B. Murphy[?]
James Hay
Elias White

Fourth--Appointed a committee of the following Brethren: James Hay, Monroe Robinson, Elias White, John Gibbs, and William Gregory to pitch a plan to fence the Graveyard, build a stand and to superintend the same and to report tomorrow. Fifth--Collected the sum of $2.46¼.

August 26, 1836. In conference met. First Delegated our Brethren William Gregory and Jason Greer as representatives to the Bethel Association and in case either fail Brother Henry Garrett to fill their place. Also appointed Brother J. Greer to write a letter also send $1.50 for printing minutes.

August 27, 1836. In conference met. and after forming a Presbytery of the following Brethren: Rev. T. S . Greer, H. McDougal, T. Ray, C. Woodruff, and A. Ray proceeded to the ordination of Brother Henry Garrett to and set him apart to the office of a Deacon.

September 24, 1836. In conference met. First--Received by experience William Purseley and received Sister Lucinder Robinson by letter.
Second--Read and received the Association letter unanimously. Third--agreed to give a public invitation to the church and congregation to make a collection to send to Burmah. Fourth Collected $4.31½ cents also agreed make a collection in November expressly for our pastor. Fifth--Gave our delegates $5.00-$2.50 each.

October 22. 1836. First--Granted Sister Susan Greer a certificate or letter of dismission.

November 1836. In conference met and dismissed Sister Ann Anderson.

December 24, 1836. In conference met. First Dismissed Brother and Sister Henry Garrett and Elizabeth wife. Second Resolve at our next meeting we let out the keeping of the house to the lowest bidder whose duty it shall be to sweep the house monthly--previous to each meeting also to keep the key of the house and to clean the spring every time the house is swept. Nevertheless if the person biding off the said house and fail in one instant to perform, or cause to be done the above specified duty, they shall forfeit all their wages. Third--Collected the sum of $4.62½.

January 21, 1837. In conference met. First--Dismissed our Sister Rachel Greer, Brother Jesse Greer and Polly Greer his wife- also Sister Sinia Jackson. Second--Let out the meeting house agreeable to the Resolution of last meeting, which was bid off by Brother Clemmons Howard at $3.50.

February 25, 1837. In conference met and Nothing done.

March 23, 1837. First--Called Brother Elias White to the office or Deacon by ballot. Second--Resolve that the first Sunday meeting be kept up. Third--- postponed a collection till the morrow.

April 22, 1837. In conference met and after prayer by T. S. Greer adjourned.

May 27, 1837. In conference met. First--Appointed a meeting to commence at this place on Friday after the fourth Sunday in July for the purpose of ordaining a deacon and communion which meeting will be protracted for several days--also agreed to send to the Padgette Creek and Upper Fairforest churches for help. Second--Took up the following query: Can professors of the Christian religion be actuated by the true principles of their profession while they take part with great interest in a conversation that is entirely vain & of this world.

Answers: The Christian may be carried into many vain conversations by company --But we believe that each diversion of that sort is a violation of His principles.

June 4, 1837. In conference met First Sunday. First Took up the consider- ation of the gift of Brother Anthony (Means) and finding it (in the opinion of the church) without growth and unprofitable, therefore resolve that he exercise no further than to sing, pray and exhort till further advised by the church. Also excluded Adam (Gist) for stealing.

June 24, 1837. In conference met. First Received by letter Nancy Greer. Second--Collected the sum of $2.75.

July 2, 1837. First Sunday in church conference met. First--Took under the watch care of this church, a negro man called Wyatt--Belonging to (Gist) also agreed to keep up the first Sunday meeting quarterly beginning the first Sunday in October.

July 21, 1837. In Conference met. Postponed the ordination of Deacon there being no help.

August 26, 1837. First--Set apart the 4 Sunday in September for the ordination of a Deacon and communion and appointed Brethren William Gregory, and Jason Greer as messengers to the Padgette Creek Church for help and Spencer Greer and M. Robinson to the Upper Fairforest for the same purpose also agreed that the committee on the Graveyard be authorized to view the old Baptistry and make what disposition of the lumber that they may think proper. Also delegated our Brethren Jason Greer and William Gregory to the Association and Brother John Gibbs in case of failure. And appointed Brother Greer to prepare a letter. Also agreed to give our delegates $2.50 each to defray their expenses and send $1.50 for printing minutes and also collection $2.50.

September 23, 1837. In conference met. First --Read and approved the Association letter. Collection $1.00

October 21, 1837. In conference met. First--postponed the ordination of deacon and also communion till at such time as the church as an opportunity of doing so. Also agreed to send Brethren M. Robinson and Spencer Bobo to cite Brother negro Anthony to answer to charges against him for endeavoring to preach without liberty of the church. Also discarded a negro man Whatt (Gist). And lastly unanimously called Elder T. Ray to supply the church as pastor.

October 22, 1837. In conference met and dismissed Brother Negro Enoch.

November 25, 1837. First--Dismissed Sisters (Negroes) Polly and Milly (Holcomb) also laid over the case of Brother Anthony and appointed Brother John Gibbs to make a special inquiry after his conduct and report to next meeting--Also took up a charge against Brother Negroe Toney for theft and departing from the truth and appointed the following Brothers W. Gregory, J. Gibbs, and M. Robinson and H. Murphy a committee to hear and examine the case and report the next meeting--and lastly presented to the ordination of a deacon Brother E. White by help of Brother Elders T. Ray and C. Duncan a presbytery.

January 27, 1838. In conference met. Took in a letter given to Negro Enoch for transgression after letter given--also took up the case of Brother Anthony but laid over till next conference and appointed Brother John Gibbs and others to consult with McMeans--Also took up the cause of Brother Toney but laid over and appointed Brother J. Greer to cite him to attend next meeting-- and lastly agreed to take up a collection tomorrow to defray the expenses of the church.

February 24, 1838. In conference met. First--Suspended the cause of Brother Anthony and appointed Brethren William Gregory and James Ray to wait on him. Second--Took up the cause of Brother Tony. He came forward and succeeded in making confession satisfactory to the church and also concluded to take a collection tomorrow and also appointed a first Sunday meeting in March.

February 25, 1838. Collected the sum of $8.75.

March 24, 1838. In conference met. First--Granted letters of dismission to Sisters Susan R. Greer, and Elizabeth Lee--Also appointed a first Sunday meeting to commence the first Sunday in April and to continue till the church discontinues it. Appointed Brethren White and J. Gibbs to labor with Brother Anthony, also a charge was brought against Brother Thomas Woodson for disorderly conduct and nonattendance at church and appointed Brethren Robinson and E. White to cite him to the church also entered a charge vs. Sister negro Minna (Rice) for dancing and agreed to call the roll at the next first Sunday meeting.

April 21 1838.. In conference met. First-- agreed to take one month to consult the scriptures on the propriety or impropriety of using private labors in public transgression also laid over the cause of Brother Thomas Woodson and appointed Brother Gregory, White, and Robinson to labour with and report at the next meeting-- also laid over the cause of Minna till first Sunday.

May 6, 1838. First Sunday in conference. Dismissed Sister negro Agnes (Clowney).

May 26, 1838. In conference met. Received the report of the committee appointed to labour with Brother Anthony, which favorable, consequently forgave him, also took up the cause of Brother T. Woodson and no satisfaction being made excluded him also excluded negro Nina (Rice). Then took up the cause relating to labour and suspended it till next meeting and also appointed the 4th Sunday in July for a communion Season. Received and answered a letter from Owensboro, Davies County, Ky.

June 23, 1838. In conference met. First dropped the question of labour unanimously and continued the old plan of discipline (as laid down in the 18th chapter of Matthew.) Also took up the question of the 8 Resolution of the last year's minutes and lastly collected the sum of $2.12½.

July 21, 1838. In conference met. First-Granted a letter of dismission to Sister Eleanor Bishop. Second-took up the question of last meeting and after much discussion laid it over for discussion at our next meeting and also took up the 9th resolution on Home Missions and laid it over till next meeting. Third-- Collected the sum of 70 cents.

August 25, 1838. In conference. First--took up the reference of last meeting on the State Convention and disapproved of the association becoming a member of the said convention unanimously. Also discarded or dropped the question on Home Missions. Second-- Delegated Brother J. Greer and W. Gregory to the Bethel Association and in case of failure Brother John Gibbs also appointed Brother J. Greer to write a letter. Gave our delegates $2.50 each and constituted $2.00 for printing minutes.

September 22, 1838. In conference met. First--Read and received the Association letter, and also collected the sum of $2.12½. (Peter applied for a letter.)

October 27, 1838. In conference met. First--dismissed our brother negro Peter (Murphy). Second--Received a letter from the Union Church requesting help to settle a difficulty there existing between Brother C. Gibbs and S. Hays--the request granted and appointed Brother J. Greer and H. Murphy to join them at their meeting an to aid in settling said difficulty. Third--postponed the calling of a minister till at our next meeting.

November 24, 1838. Received the report of the Brethren sent to the Union Church which was (in purport) to lay Brother Gibbs and wife and Brother Hays all under a sensure till they can become reconciled to each other and agreed to wait with them till next meeting. Second--called Elder T. Ray to supply us for the next year also took a collection for our said pastor for the last year. Third--received the report of a committee on Graveyard with an offer of Brother C. Gibbs of $13.60.

December 22, 1838. In conference met. First--dismissed our Sister Sarah M. Greer also from a request of the church in Tennessee restored a colored man John (Harlin) and granted him a letter. Second-- Took up the cause of Brother C. Gibbs and after much discussion laid it over till the next meeting.

Sunday 23. Collected the sum of $3.00

January 26, 1839. In conference met. First--hearing a favorable report of the difficulty existing between Brethren Gibbs and Hays but none of the parties being present, we continued the cause till next meeting. Second--appointed a committee of the following Brethren J. Gibbs and J. Hay and H. B. Murphy to project and superintend the repairing of the church yard and to appoint a day on which they may have a public working.

February 23. In conference met. First--Granted letters of dismission to sister Clary Little and Brother Spencer Greer. Also took up the cause of Brother Gibbs and Hays. Brother Gibbs stated that the difficulty intimately settled--consequently we discarded the same.

March. Nothing done.

April 27, 1839. In conference met. First-- concluded to take a collection tomorrow for the purpose of the church.

Sunday 28. Collected $1.93 3/4.

MINUTES OF LOWER FAIRFOREST BAPTIST CHURCH

May 25, 1839. In conference met. First-- Received a request from Upper Fairforest asking help to settle a difficulty between Brethren Rountree and Palmer. The request was granted and we sent Brethren John Gibbs, James Hay, William Gregory, Jason Greer and Hyram Murphy.

June 22. In conference met. First-- Received a certificate from Mr. William P. Graham certifying to the good character of a negro named Henry (Robinson) and we appointed Brethren J. Hay to correspond with said Graham by letter in which he is to give the charges for which the said Henry was excluded.

July 27, 1839. In conference met. First--dismissed Sister Martha Y. Guinn. Second- A charge brought against Brother James Woodson for nonattendance at conference and appointed Brother M. Robinson to call on him for his reason for the same. Third--collected the sum of $3.50 also directed our clerk to purchase a lock for the church door.

August 24, 1839. In conference met. First--Brother Churchill Gibbs came forward and made an acknowledgment in which he states that he has been exceedingly wrong and begs that the Church would bear with him till the next meeting, in consequence of which the church appointed a committee of Brethren J. Greer, J. Hay, and W. Gregory to aid the parties in reconcilliation.

Dismissed our sister, Harriet Fincher by letter. Received the report Br. Robinson which gave the church entire satisfaction with Brother James Woodson also the church agreed to continue the first Sunday meeting and also delegated Brother W. Gregory and Jason Greer and in case of failure Brother James Hay to represent us in the Bethel Association and appointed Brother Jason Greer to prepare a letter to said body and send $2.00 for the printing of the minutes and lastly collected the sum of 50 cents.

September 21, 1839. First--Brother William Presley came forward and made a confession in which he states that he has been far out of the way and craves to be forgiven, his acknowlegment and read and he was forgiven. Second-- Read the report of the committee of labour which leave both Brethren Robinson and Gibbs both under a sensure--the former in one degree and the latter in two degrees of error but the church waits with them till the next. Third-- Dismissed Sister Susan R. Greer by letter. Fourth--Read and approved the Association letter and also collected the sum of $2.25.

October 26, 1839. In conference met. First--dismissed Sister Mary Fincher by letter. Second--Heard the acknowledgment of Brother Robinson and Gibbs which gave general satisfaction to the church therefore, they were both restored to fellowship again. Third-- charge brought against negro Anthony for passing the limits give him by the church and appointed Brethren Robinson and Gibbs to cite him to the first Sunday meeting in Nov.

November-- no meeting in consequence of bad weather.

November 27. In conference met and dismissed Brother Robert Woodson by letter.

January 25, 1840. In conference met and took up the cause of Brother negro Anthony and agreed to refer the case to the first Sunday meeting in February. Second-- Received Brother Joshua Wilborn by letter.

February 22, 1840. Conference met. First--Dismissed by letter Sister Priscilla Browning--then took up the cause of negro Anthony and whereas the church being satisfied that he does not subject himself to their government and is persistening in a cause by them forbidden (for taking a text and attempting to preach) therefore, resolve that if he makes no satisfaction on or by the next meeting the church will proceed to his exclusion. Third--collected the sum of $6.00 for pastor and called Elder T. Ray to supply the next year unanimously. Collected 25 cents for sweeping by Brother Hay.

March 21, 1840. W. Walker preached. In conference met, but no preaching. First the report of Brethren Gregory and White the purpose of which was that the condition of the roof of our church required our immediate attention, but dropt the consideration. Second-- Collected the sum of $4.25 and paid over to Br. Hay $5.18 3/4 it being the ballance on act. Third--appointed Brother Gregory to inquire into an unfavorable report against Negro Jim (Murphy) and to report it next meeting.

April 25, 1840. In conference met, and dismissed by letter Brother Elder J. C. Thurber. Second-- Took up the report of the committee on recovering meeting House but considering the busy season of the year--concluded to suspend any further proceedings on matters till next meeting in June. Third--Negro Jim came forward and acknowledged being guilty of sin of in toxication--but made such concessions as gave the church general satisfaction. Fourth-Hearing an unfavorable report of Negro Abram (Palmer) we request Brother J. Gibbs to cite him to our next meeting to answer to said report.

May 25, 1840. In conference met. W. Walker preached. First--appointed a committee of Brethren Gregory, Greer, Robinson, White, and H. B. Murphy to wait on negro Abram tomorrow and report at our next meeting.

June 27. First--Agreed to let the committee stand and wait on Abram tomorrow. Second-- in regard to the reference of April meeting. We agreed that Brother Greer drew a subscription (payable in Dec. next.) for the purpose of recovering our meeting house and that Brethren Gregory, White and Gibbs and H. B. Murphy, and James Hay appointed to hold subscription and superintend the said work.

Sunday 28. The committee appointed to wait on Abram-- finding no proof to sustain the charges against the said Abram--exempted him from said charges.

July 25, 1840. In conference met. Heard and acknowledged of our old brother Joshua Greer which was unanimously received and he was restored to fellowship after an absence of 25 years. Second--Delegated Brethren Gregory and Greer to the Association and in case of failure appointed Brother John Gibbs. Also appointed Br. J. Greer to prepare a letter for the same. Third-- appointed our next meeting to be a communion season. Fourth--Collected the sum of $1.12½ concluded to give Br. Walker $4.00 for his services with us, and ordered Br. J. Greer to hand it over to him.

August--Nothing done.

September-- Nothing done.

October 24, 1840. In conference met. Sister Lucinda Robinson applied for a letter, but Br. J. Gibbs objected to her having one, consequently the matter was deferred to our next meeting. Second--Appointed our next meeting to commence on Friday before the 4th Sunday in November next and a communion on Sunday.

October 25. Received by experience negro Dinah (Beaty).

November 20. In conference met. First--the difficulty of Br. John Gibbs and Sister Lucinda Robinson settled and consequently by Sister Robinson receiving a letter. Second--The church appointed Br. H. B. Murphy to call on Elder T. Ray to inform us when they as a church have failed to treat him as a minister. Unanimously called Elder D. Duncan to supply us.

November 21. Received a letter of Sister Lueza Humphries.

December 1840. In conference met. First--Heard the report of Br. H. B. Murphy and unanimously agreed to drop any further inquiry or labour in the case. Second--agreed to commence working on the meeting house on the 2nd Monday in January next. Third--agreed to unanimously that the neighborhood be at liberty to build a school house on the church land at this place.

January 23, 1841. In conference met--Brother Roberts preached. First-- Received a request from Padgett Creek Church requesting help in a difficulty and we sent Brethren Joshua Greer, E. White and H. B. Murphy.

February 27, 1841. In conference met. First--Unanimously called Brother James Roberts to supply the church.

March 27, 1841. In conference met. First--Brother William Presley and wife applied for letters of dismission, but there being some objections to Brother William Presley deferred it till our next meeting.

April 2, 1841. In conference met, and agreed to let the covering of the half of the meeting house out tomorrow to the lowest bidder.

April 25, 1841. Brother C. Gibbs agreed to perform the above specified work for the sum of eight dollars paid in two months.

May 22, 1841. In conference. First--Dismissed Sister Letitha Presley by letter. Second--requested Brother Hay to inform Brother Presley that there was dissatisfaction in the church respecting his past conduct and therefore requested him to appear at our next meeting.

May 23. Baptised 2 colored persons.

June 26. 1841. Brother Presley came forward and gave satisfaction in the church respecting his past conduct, and therefore obtained a letter of dismission. Second--Took up the 9th resolution of the Bethel Association and unanimously disapproved of the said association becoming a member of convention.

July 24, 1841. In conference met. The committee appointed to recover the meeting house returned all their business it being completed. Second--Agreed to meet on Friday 6th of August to recover shed. Third--also delegated Brother J. Greer and William Gregory to the Bethel Association and in case of failure Brethren John Gibbs and James Hay also appointed Br. J. Greer to prepare a letter to the said body--We also agree to send two dollars for the minutes. Fourth --Resolve to commence our meeting on Friday to have a communion on Sunday and to take up a collection on same day for general purposes.

August 21, 1841. In conference met. First--Dismissed Sister Elizabeth Woodson. Second--Received and appraised the Association letter also collected the sum of $3.12½. Third--Agreed to meet on Friday before the fourth Sunday in September to cover the shed.

August 22. Dismissed negro William Grimke.

August 3. Received by experience Mary Willard.

September 14. Received by experience Susan Clark.

October 23, 1841. In conference met and at the request of New Hope church. We restored Negro John (Harlin) and Philip (Bryant) and granted them letters of dismission. Second--Agreed to meet on Tuesday next and let out the covering the shed to the lowest bidder.

October 24, 1841. In conference met and restored Negro Bill (McBeth).

Tuesday 25--The work went off at four dollars and 37½ cents to John White. Paid it November meeting.

November 26, 1841. In conference met. First--Brother James Woodson and wife requested letters of dismission but there being objections against him for intemperence--suspended his but granted his wife a letter. Also granted letters of dismission to Brother Gregory and wife.

December 1841. The work was let out to Benj. White $5.00.

January 27, 1842. In conference met. Brother Duncan preached and the church agreed to take a collection for Br. Roberts.

February 26, 1842. In conference met and agreed to go into an election for deacons at our next meeting. Election of Brother H. B. Murphy singing clerk. Brother Bird Murphy and wife solicited the church to take them under their watch care. The church suspended the same for consideration till our next meeting. Agreed that services should commence on Saturday and Sunday at 11 O'clock.

March 24, 1842. In conference met. First--Brother Joshua Greer came forward with an acknowledgement in which he states that he had been far out of the way and craved the prayers and forgiveness of the church which was granted him. Second--Elected by ballott Brethren H. B. Murphy and John Gibbs to the office of deacon and suspended any further proceeding on the matter for brethren elected to consider the matter and to give a final answer at our next meeting. Third--unanimously agreed to take brother Bird Murphy and wife under the watch care of the church. Fourth--appointed a committee of Brethren H. B. Murphy, James Hay, and John Gibbs to wait on Anthony tomorrow and report to the church.

April 23, 1842. In conference met. First--Brethren H. B. Murphy and John Gibbs same forward and agreed to serve the church as Deacons. We then agreed to send for help in order that their ordination shall take place the Saturday before the 4th Sunday in June and communion on Sunday. Second-- Received an unfavorable report of Anthony therefore left him where we found him.

May 21, 1842. In conference met. First--Agreed to let the matter of Brother James Woodson rest till our meeting in August next.

June 25, 1842. In conference met. First took up the case of our deacons, the help not being present agreed to send for the same viz. Elder Walker, Kindricks and John Jeter, and postponed the ordination as well as the communion till Saturday before the 4th Sunday in July conference to be held Friday before. Second-- Granted letters of dismission to Brother John Murrell and to negro Mary (Mitchell). Third Received a letter from Padgett Creek asking an explanation of our object in receiving some persons under our watch-care whom the had excluded. We agreed to write and for that purpose appointed the following committee to write viz; J. Greer, John Gibbs, I. P. Murphy, E. White, and M. Robinson also appointed J. Greer, I. P. Murphy and John Gibbs to bear it. Fourth. Took into consideration the gift of Brother Joshua Greer we allowed him to preach till our next meeting. We say how far his liberties shall extend.

July 22, 1842. In conference met. First heard from the Brethren bearing our answer to the Padgett Creek which was received as far as they were conserned with general satisfaction. We then took up the case of the gift of Brother Joshua Greer, but suspended it till tomorrow. Delegated our Brother J. Greer and John Gibbs and in case of failure H. B. Murphy and I. P. Murphy. Appointed Brother J. Greer to prepare a letter to the Bethel Association. We all agreed to send $2.00 for printing minutes and to take a collection for that purpose at our next meeting. We also appointed the 15th day of August and days following to work on stand and camp ground. The church hearing an unfavorable report of Brother William Pressley of disorderly conduct-- appointed Brethren J. Wilborn, Robert Boatman to cite him at our next meeting. Fourth. We received a letter from Padgett Creek Church, but suspended the consideration of it till tomorrow.

July 23. In conference. The Brethren elders W. Walker, D. Duncan, and J. Kindricks by request attended and organized a presbytary to proceed to the ordination of our brethren John Gibbs and Hyram B. Murphy as Deacons. Second. Took up the case of Brother Joshua Greer and decided that he exercise his gifts in prayer and exhortation and preaching. Third. Took up the letter from Padgett Creek, but being informed by our representatives that there were doubts concerning our answer being the act of the church. We appointed our former representatives viz. J. Greer, I. P. Murphy, and John Gibbs to attend the next meeting of the Padgett Creek Church and to declare to them orally that the letter which we sent the special act of our church and to refer them to that for our answer to them, second, and that there were no difference of opinion that we would discern among us on the subject which they allude.

August 27, 1842. In conference met. First. Read and received the Association letter then took up a collection of $3.25 also appointed the Monday before the Association to complete the work of our preparation for the meeting of that body. Second. Heard the report of Brother Wilburn he states that he saw Brother Presley and he said that it was his failing to drink. We agree to wait on him till next meeting he not being present. Third. the report of the Brethren sent to Padgett Creek they say that they delivered their message and that by an act of the church their answer was not received satisfactory. Fourth. The church then made a call for a pastor for the next year and found that Elder Duncan was the unanimous choice. He did not answer to said call, but said that he would in due time. Lastly we agreed that our next conference be held Friday before the commencement of the Association.

September 23, 1842. In conference met took up the case of Brother James Woodson but laid it over till December, also took up the case of Brother Presley and laid it over till October meeting.

MINUTES OF LOWER FAIRFOREST BAPTIST CHURCH

October 22, 1842. In conference met. Took up the case of Br. Presley and after hearing a favorable report of him concluded to continue our unity towards him till December.

November 26. Proceeded to take a collection for Br. Duncan the result of which was $25.25 which was accordingly handed to him. Br. Duncan consented to serve as supply pastor the ensuing year.

December 24, 1842. In conference met. First took up the case of Brother James Woodson, he being present made an acknowledgment that gave the church satisfaction, consequently gave him a letter of dismission and also a letter to his wife hers being lost. Second. Took up the cause of Br. Presley he not being present, excluded him and also requested Br. Hay to say to Sister Presley to return her letter or put it into some other church.

January 7, 1843. Conference nothing done.

February 25, 1843. In conference met. Resolve that we have a communion meeting twice a year i. e. May and August and that our meeting on those occasions commence on Friday before and that our Brethren be requested to invite ministers and members of other churches to attend said meeting.

March 25, 1843, In conference met. First received Sister Presley's letter which we had given her 22 of May 1841. Also took a collection for the purpose of the church say about $1.70 cts.

April 22 1843. In conference met. First: received from Br. Hay 50 cents for the purpose of the church.

May 26, 1843. Nothing done that required a minute.

May 27, 1843. Received by experience Nancy and Elizabeth Sparks.

May 28, 1843. Received by experience Thomas Hart also G. S. Nolin's negro woman Eliza such for membership she being long since baptized deferred till our next administration [of] the Lord's Supper.

June 24, 1843. In conference met. First: Took up the case of Eliza (Nolin) and appointed Br. J. Greer to examine into her case and report at our next meeting. Second: Br. Hay was admonished by the church for his objecting publickly to Br. A. Ray's preaching. He acknowledged that he was sorry if he had hurt the feelings of any of the brethren or anybody for he done it from his own feelings, and took the responsibility on himself and did not wish or intend to involve the church in any difficulty whatever. His acknowledgement received.

July 22, 1843. In conference met. First: he read the report of Br. J. Greer in reference to Negro Eliza's case and referred it to a Committee of the whole church to hear her on the morrow and report at our meeting. Second: Delegated Brethren J. Greer and J. Gibbs to the Bethel Association and in case of failure Brethren I. P. Murphy and James Hay. Also appointed Br. J. Greer to write to said body and request Br. I. P. Murphy to assist him.

August 25, 1843. In conference met. First: Took up the case of Eliza referred to a committee at our last meeting, but our preacher not being present we laid it over till the morrow. Second: Read and received the Association letter and unanimously called Br. D. Duncan to supply the ensuing year also agreed to send two dollars for the printing of the minutes. Lastly collected the sum of $3.00 for the purpose of the church.

August 26, 1843. In conference met. First. Received by letter Brother David Holcomb, deacon, and Dicey Holcomb his wife. Second: Took up Eliza's case and received her as restored.

September 1843. Association prevented our meeting.

October 1847. In conference met and nothing done that would require Minutes.

November 1843. In conference met and Br. Elder D. Duncan agreed to attend us the ensuing year.

December 23, 1843. In conference met. Br. I. P. Murphy moderator heard the report of the delegates from the Association and appointed the following committee Brethren J. Greer, I. P. Murphy, J. Gibbs, James Hay, and C. Gibbs to take into consideration the said report and the minutes of the Bethel Association and to report at our next meeting. Second: collected the sum of $16.50 for the benefit of our supply, D. Duncan.

January, 1844. No meeting in consequence of the inclement weather.

February 24, 1844. In conference met. First: received Br. Samuel Harlin by letter. Second: received the report of tire committee with Sunday resolutions which was unanimously adopted, also agreed to transmit a copy of said resolutions to the different churches belonging to the Bethel Association.

Copy of the Resolutions

Whereas the Bethel Association has (in our opinion) committed several irregularities and constitutional errors therefore resolve:

1: That we feel ourselves agrieved at the cause of the Bethel Association at our meeting in 1843 in more particulars than one, but especially in regard to our sister, the Newhope church.

2: Resolve that we intend to use the proper means within our power to reclaim s'd association to order and conform to her constitution.

3: Resolve that in order to effect the purpose of the foregoing resolution as far as it may, we intend in our next annual address to the said association to point out what we think to be the irregularities of said association with which we are agrieved.

4: Resolve that as we consider the cause of s'd association at her meeting in 1843 with regard to the Newhope Church to be unconstitutional with few exceptions. We hereby say that we recognize her the said church as occupying precisely in point of constitutional order in relation to us and the association the station she did when her delegates took their seats in the association in 1842.

Third: Prepared a charge against Sister Holly Sparks for fornication and after due deliberation excluded her. Also agreed that at our next meeting to take collection for the use of the church and to continue to quarterly as been our custom to do.

March 1844. No meeting.

April 27, 1844. In conference met. First: Took up a collection as it was omitted at our last meeting the result of which was $2.37½ cents. Second: Also agreed that at our meeting in May our meeting commence on Friday and a communion on Sunday.

May 2, 1844. Elder Jacks preached from the 27 psalm and 4 verse. In conference and appointed the following Br. J. Greer, I. P. Murphy, J. Gibbs, H. B. Murphy and J. Hay a committee whose duty it is to apoint out what we conceive those of the Bethel Association as mentioned in our minutes of February last and to report at our next meeting.

June 22, 1844. In conference met. Called for the report of the committee appointed at our last and after some discussion postponed it till our next.

July 27, 1844. In conference met. First: Took up the report of the committee which was adopted. Second: Delegated I. P. Murphy and J. Greer to the Bethel Association and J. Gibbs and J. Hay as alternated also appointed Br. J. Greer to write and send $2.00 for minutes.

August 23, 1844. In conference met. Received two letters one from the Hopewell Church and the other from the Brushy Fork.

August 24, 1844. In conference met. First: Received the association letter unanimously. Second: Collected the sum of two dollars and 45 cents for general purposes. Third: Unanimously called Elder D. Duncan to supply as the ensuing year also agreed to pay Br. John Gibbs seven dollars for 2000 shingles that was put on the shed. Fourth: Preferred a charge against sister Polly Willard for fornication, the facts being proven proceeded to exclude her. Lastly agreed to make a collection for our supply in October next.

October 27, 1844. In conference met. Elder D. Duncan consented to serve the church the ensuing year as a supply. Collected the sum of $17.35 for expressed purpose of our supply.

November 1844. No transaction of the church that requires a minute.

December 1844. Nothing done.

March 22, 1844. In Conference met and nothing of importance was transacted by the church.

April 1844. In conference met. The church proposed having a meeting to commence at this place on Friday before the 4th Sunday in July next. Several ministers from a distance is expected to be here at that time.

May 24, 1845. In conference met. First: Resolved that Br. Hay repair one of the windows of this house and report the cost at our next.

June 21, 1845. In conference met. First: Agreed to pay Br. Hay $0.81 cents for a new blind to a window. Second: Granted letters of dismission to Negroes Enoch and Jesse (Wilborn). Third: Collected the sum of $1.22 cents.

Sunday June 25, 1845. Received by letter negroe Jesse (B. Lyles).

July 25, 1845. First: Requested Br. J. Greer to write to the Catawba Church concerning a colored man Whyat. Second: Delegated Brethren I. P. Murphy and J. Greer to the Bethel Association in case of failure Br. J. Gibbs and J. Hay and Br. I. P. Murphy to write John Calhoun Russell.

August 23, 1845. In conference met. First: Granted a letter of dismission to Sister Sarah White. Second: Read and received the association letter--also agreed to send two dollars for minutes and for that purpose collected one dollar and 50 cents. Lastly unanimously called Elder D. Duncan to supply us the ensuing year.

September 1845. Disappointed by the association.

October 1845. No conference.

November 22, 1845. In conference met. Brother I. P. Murphy was called to the chair --Brother Harlin prayed the church then appoint Brethren Greer and I. P. Murphy, H. B. Murphy and D. Holcomb messengers to the proposed convention of the churches at Cane Creek with instructions to write their own letter based on the following resolutions who are also instructed to invite the Bethel Association to hold an extra session with us if they come to such a conclusion. Resolve that this church so far as she is concerned with the association retain the same constitution and order of the Bethel Association. And lastly collected the sum of seven dollars and 50 cents for our pastor.

December 27, 1845. In conference met. Elder Jacks preached Elder D. Duncan being gone to the West--the church proceeded to a second call for a minister which resulted in the unanimous call of Brother W. W. Guin to supply us the ensuing year.

January 7, 1846.

February 7, 1846.

March 1846. Nothing done.

May 22, 1846. Took up a collection of $1.20 cts and requested the clerk write Elder E. Fant to come up to our three day meeting in August, Communion &c.

June 27, 1846. In conference met. Brother Jacks preached. Granted a letter of dismission to Br. A. M. Robinson. Collected 75 cents.

July 25, 1846. In conference met, 1: received by letter Sister Elener Comer. 2: Received the report of the treasurer. 3: Delegated Br. J. Greer, I. P. Murphy to the Bethel Association and in case of failure Br. J. Hay and Robert Boatman and also requested the clerk to prepare a letter to the Association.

August 21, 1846. In conference met. Elder Kendricks preached. First: Granted a letter of dismission to sister Nancy Johns. Second: Agreed to send for minutes $2.00 also read and received the Association letter and also collected the Sum of $3.12½ for home missions and $1.35 for general purposes. Third: Preferred a charge against Br. Joshua Wilborn for Fornification and after a thorough examination of the matter excluded him.

September 1846. Disappointed by Association.

October 24, 1846. In conference met. Granted letters of dismission to Brother Elias White and Ann White his wife and Samuel Harlin.

November 21, 1846. In conference met. 1st: Received by confession of faith Bird Murphy, Jepeth Murphy and Nancy his wife, Wiley Murphy and his wife Nancy. 2nd: Called Elder M. C. Barnet to supply this church the ensuing year. J. Greer, Clk.

December 26, 1846. In conference met. First: Received by confession of faith Sister Charlotte Duncan and Sylvia Murphy. Second: Collected the sum of $2.46¼. J. Greer, Clerk.

January 16, 1847. In conference met. Whereas at our first Meeting we changed our time of meeting, for the purpose of obtaining the services of Elder M. C. Barnet as a supply but he has since declined the said call, Therefore resolved that we change our days of preaching to the original time, the fourth Sabbath. J. Greer, Clerk.

February 27, 1847. In conference met. First: Unanimously called Elder M. C. Owens to supply this church the present year. Second: preferred charges against negro, Jim (Murphy) for disorderly conduct and appointed Br. Hay, Greer, and Jepthe Murphy a committee to wait on him tomorrow and to report at our next meeting. J. Greer, Clerk.

March 27, 1847. In conference met. First: received a letter from Sister Martha Ann Hodges. Second: received the report of the committee to wait on Jim which was in amount to retain him in fellowship. Third: collected the sum of $1.90 and also on Sunday .10 also which makes $2.00. J. Greer, Clerk.

April 24, 1847. In conference met. First: agreed to gave a communion meeting in May, commencing on Friday.

Sunday 25. Received by confession of Faith Susan Murphy and negro Julia (Nolin) by experience. J. Greer, Clerk.

May, Friday 21, 1847. In conference met. First: in consequence of an unfavorable report of J. Nix (Nolin) we appoint Br. Hay and Greer a committee to inquire Into the matter and report at our next.

Saturday 22. Received by letter Sister Mariah Black.

Sunday 23. Received by confession of Faith Brother Harrison Baley and sister Margaret Baley. J. Greer, Clerk

June 26, 1847. In conference met. First: appointed a meeting on the first Sunday in July for the benefit of the Black People. Second: agreed to pay Br. Hay one dollar for putting in a trunk[?] in our spring.

July 24, 1847. In conference met. First: received by confession of faith Brother John C. Bobo. Second: received the report of the committee to inquire into the charges against Julia which was favorable to her and cleared her of all charges. Third: collected the sum of $2.75 for general purposes. Fourth: Delegated Br. J. Greer, I. P. Murphy and James Hay to the Bethel Association and Br. J. Gibbs alternate--also requested Br. Greer to write and also to send $3.00 for minutes.

MINUTES OF LOWER FAIRFOREST BAPTIST CHURCH

July 25, 1847. Received by experience Negro Polly (Bogan).

August 21, 1847. In conference met. First: received by confession Br. Sherwood Dukes also negro Alsey (Gist). Second: Resolve that our next meeting be on Thursday and Friday before the fourth in September next. J. Greer, Clerk

September 25, 1847. In conference met. Unanimously called Elder M. C. Owings to supply this church for the ensuing year.

November 27, 1847. In conference met. First: Took up a collection of fifty three dollars and 50 cents for our supply. Second: granted letters of dismission to Brother Jeptha Murphy and sister Nancy Murphy his wife. Third: Agreed that the first Sunday in Dec. be set apart for a meeting place at this place for the black people.

December 25, 1847. First: Received under the watch care of this church a colored man George (Jones) also continued the first Sunday meeting.

January 22, 1848. In conference met no act of the church requiring a minute.

Sunday 23. Received by confession of Faith Sister Susan Beaty-- Also received by experience Negro Edmond (Rice), also restored Henry (Beaty).

February 26, 1848. in conference met and nothing of Importance transacted.

March 25, 1848. In conference met. Collected the sum of $1.55 for general Purposes.

April 22, 1848. In conference met and received by letter Sister Sarah Norman. Collected 50 cents for general purposes--Adjourned.

May 26, 1848. In conference met. Nothing done.

May 28, 1848. Sunday received by letter Br. George (Jones).

June 1848. Nothing done

July 22, 1846. In conference met. First: received by confession of faith Sister Nancy Bobo. Second: Delegated Brother I. P. Murphy, and J. Hay to the Bethel Association, and in case of failure Brother J. Gibbs, H. B. Murphy and Greer to prepare a letter with instructions to invite the association to sit with us at her next meeting. Collected the sum of $2.40 appointed Brother J. Gibbs and J. Hay, J. Greer, and D. Holcomb a committee to examine our boundaries of church land and report at our next. Adjourned-J. Greer, C. C.

August 25, 1846. In conference met. Elder Cheak preached. First: Sister Mary Gibbs presented a letter of dismission craving fellowship and after considerable discussion it vias postponed till some future period. Second: Read and adopted the resolution letter. Third: Agreed to send $3.00 for printing minutes and $1.50 on the same last year. Also agreed to take up a collection fund for the education on Sunday of the Bethel Association. Fourth: appointed Brothers J. P. Murphy, J. Norman and J. Gibbs a committee to arrange preaching through the present meeting. Adjourned. J. Greer, C. C.

August 26, 1848. Granted a letter of dismission to Sister Lydia Kitchens.

August 27, 1848. Collected for tire Association Education Fund $5.00.

August 29, 1846. Received by experience, William B. Murphy, and Susan Sparks.

August 29, 1848. Received by experience Sister Milly White, Charlotte Tucker, and a colored woman, Finder (H. B. Murphy's).

August 30, 1848. Received by experience Brother, John Hay and Sister Nancy White. Restored negro Disey (Prince).

August 31, 1848. James Greer, George Harlin, Sister Jane Howard, Julia Murphy, Susan Murphy, Malissa Harlin, Susan Smith, Milly Sanders, Margaret Bailey came in by experience.

September 1, 1848. First: received by experience Eliza (Murphy) Second: Received by experience--Brother Jesse Sparks and Sister Parry Lawson, Agreed that our next meeting be held Wednesday before the next fourth Sunday. Received by confession of faith Brother Otha Willbanks. Third: Sunday In conference. Received by experience Caroline Sparks.

September 20, 1848. In conference met. Received by confession of faith Brethren Jeremiah Bobo, Manly Bobo, and Sisters Rebecca Bobo and Mary Bobo--Also received by experience Sister Amy Ogles and Permelia C. Bobo.

October 20, 1848. In conference met. First: Appointed Brother Greer to draw a subscription to be presented tomorrow for the special pulpit supply. Second: unanimously called Elder M. C. Owings to supply this church the ensuing year.

October 21, 1848. In conference met. First: Granted a letter of dismission to Brother James Greer. Also admitted Sister Amy Ogles to Baptism.

November 25, 1848. In conference met. First: agreed that our first Sunday meeting be discontinued (In consequence of the cold season) till at such time as the church may think proper for it to recommence. J. Greer, Clerk.

December 23, 1848. In conference met. There being nothing done that require a minute--adjourned. J. Greer, Clerk.

January 27, 1849. In conference met. First: dismissed by letter our colored Brother Sam property of Wallace.

January 28, Sunday, 1849. Received by experience a coloured man Adam (Nolan) also received by confession of faith a coloured woman Mary (Rice).

February 24. In conference met-- nothing done. J.C. Bobo, Clerk protem.

March 23, 1849. In conference met. First: Received by letter Brother C. C. Vaughn a licensed preacher and Sister M. Vaughn his Wife. Also dismissed Sister Amy Ogles. J. Greer, C. C.

April 21, 1849. In conference met. First: received by experience Sisters Nancy P. Bobo and Eleanor Tucker. Second: Granted to Brother J. L. Norman a license to preach and exercise his gift when ever the Lord in His Providence may call him. Adjourned. J. Greer, Clerk.

May 25, 1849. In conference met. Brother J. L. Norman, Moderator. First: Took up the case of Sister Gibbs letter--dropt the letter and received her on confession of Faith. Second: agreed that the first Sunday meeting for the colored people be appointed to commence on the first Sunday in June next. Adjourned, J. Greer, C. C.

May 26, 1849. In conference met and restored Sarah M. Greer.

Sunday 26. In conference met and received by experience negro Julia (Murphy).

June 23, 1849. In conference met. First: Received by experience. J. S. Bobo. Adjourned J. Greer, C. C.

Sunday 24, 1849. In conference met and restored negro Anthony to the fellowship of the church but restricted him to live a private member. J. Greer, C. C.

July 1, 1849. In conference met. First: received by experience Elizabeth Robinson. Second: Granted letters of dismission to the following persons with a view of Constituting themselves into a new church. Harrison Baley, J. C. Bobo, J. S. Bobo, Margaret Baley, Mary Bobo, Mary Dukes, Rebecca Bobo, Mary Sparks, Susan D. Baley, Margaret Dukes, A. C. Bobo, Nancy B. Bobo, Jeremiah Bobo, Sherwood Dukes, Manley Bobo, Jesse Sparks, Otho Willbanks. Third: Delegated J. Greer, J. P. Murphy and J. Gibbs and as alternates H. B. Murphy and J. L. Norman. Brother Greer to prepare a letter with J. C. Bobo to assist for the Association. Fourth: Collected the sum of $3.41. Fifth: Appointed a committee on repairs of Graveyard and resolved that the first Sunday meeting cease after the next appointment. Sixth and Seventh: a charge was preferred against Sister Julia (Nolin) for departing from her husband and marrying again and appointed Brethren H. B. Murphy to cite her the next to the next meeting first Sunday. Adjourned J. Greer, C. C.

July 22, 1849. In conference met. First: appointed Brethren J. Gibbs, J. Greer, and J. Hay a committee to superintend the working at the stand.

August 24, 1849. In conference met. First: Took up the case of Julia (Nolin) and after a fair investigation of her conduct excluded her. J. L. Norman, Mod., J. Greer, C. C.

August 25, 1849. In conference. First: Read and adopted the church letter. Second: Agreed to work on the stand Friday before the third Sunday in September. Third: Collected the sum of one dollar and 75 cents for general purposes. J. Greer, C.C.

August 26, 1849. In conference. First: Received by experience, Rody Murrel.

August 27. Received by experience George W. Nance.

August 28. Dismissed Brother David Holcomb and Dicey Holcomb his wife by letter.

September 22, 1849. The Association convend with us.

September 24. In conference met and received by experience B. F. Rogers.

October 27, 1849. In conference met and unanimously called Elder M. C. Owings to supply the church the ensuing year. Also agreed to take up a subscription for our supply for the last year. James Hay, Clerk

November 24, 1849. In conference met. First: Received by experience Telitha Lawson, Mary Sparks and John Sparks. Also restored Sister Holly Sparks. Second: Granted a letter of dismission to Sister Parry Lawson. Third: Received a request from the New Prospect Church asking us to set apart Brother J. L. Norman and C. C. Vaughan to the work of the ministry, and After a prayerful consultation unanimously agreed to comply with the request as far as it relates to Brother Norman, But Brother Vaughan being absent the consideration of that part of the request relating to himself was postponed indefinitely. Adjourned. J. Greer, C. C.

December 22. 1849. In conference met. First: received Sister Jane Gibbs by letter. Second: Agreed to ordain Brother Vaughan and set him apart to the ministry and that the Saturday before the fifth Sunday in March be set apart for the purpose of the ordination of Brothers Norman and Vaughan--and that Elders Fant, Felder, Newlin, Kitchens, W. Demans and Owings are requested to attend. J. Greer, C. C.

MINUTES OF LOWER FAIRFOREST BAPTIST CHURCH

January 26, 1850. In conference met. First: Dismissed Sister Jane Rogers and Brother Franklin Rogers. Second: Appointed Brother J. Gibbs, H. B. Murphy and J. W. Murphy to a committee to employ a suitable person to keep and sweep the church at this place for one year. J. Greer, C. C.

Sunday, January 27, 1850. Received by experience a negro Charlotte (Rogers).

February 23, 1850. In conference met. First: The house committee report that they have given the case of the House to Brother Robert Boatman and that he receive one dollar and 50 cents for his years services. Second: Resolved that the church meet Friday before the fifth Sunday in March to fast and pray in consideration of the ordination on the succeeding day. Adjourned J. Greer, C. C.

March 27, 1850. In conference met. Brother Vaughan Moderator. First: granted letter of dismission to Sister Sarah M. Greer. Adjourned, J. Greer, C. C.

March 30, 1850. Elders J. L. Kindricks and M. C. Owings met formed themselves into a Presbytery and proceeded to the ordination of Brethren J. L. Norman and C. C. Vaughan setting them apart to the great work of the ministry.

April 27, 1850. In conference met-- Brother Norman, Moderator--nothing done that required a minute.

May 25, 1850. In conference met--nothing done worthy of a minute.

June 22, 1850. In conference met. First: agreed that our meeting in August be protracted just so long as the circumstances and prospects will justify. J. Greer, C. C.

July 27, 1850. In conference met. Elder Cheak, mod., First: delegated Brethren J. Greer, J, Gibbs, and I. P. Murphy and in case of failure Brethren J. L. Norman and C. C. Vaughn and J. Greer --Also agreed to send $2.00 for the printing of the minutes. Adjourned, J. Greer, C. C.

August 23, 1850. In conference met. First: Granted a letter of dismission to Sister Nancy Bobo.

August 27, 1850. Received and adopted the association letter.

September 19, 1850. In conference met. Resolved that Brother John Gibbs be permitted to exercise his gift as he may have liberty. J. Greer, C. C.

September 28, 1850. In conference met. First: Granted a letter of dismission to Sisters Susan Smith and Polly Estes. Second: In as much as the negro

45

woman Charlotte (Rogers) has been guilty of immoral conduct since she was received by experience we now discard her from the notice of the church. J. Greer, C. C.

October 27, 1850. In conference met and agreed that Brother Gibbs take up a subscription in favour of our supply for the last years services. Adjourned J. Greer, C. C.

November 23, 1850. In conference met. 1st: agreed to go into a call for the ensuing year, and after some discussion postponed It till out next meeting. Adjourned J. Greer, C. C.

December 21, 1850. In conference met. 1st: received by letter Brother J. C. Bobo, also dismissed Sisters Caroline Bishop and Susan Bishop. 2nd: Unanimously called Elder M. C. Owings to supply the church the ensuing year. 3: Collected the sum of two dollars and 75 cents for General purposes. 4: Let the keeping and sweeping for the house to Brother Robert Boatman for the sum of one dollar and fifty cents for one year. 5: Excluded Sister Susan Sparks for fornification. Owings, Mod. J. Greer. C. C.

January 7, 1851. In conference met and nothing done.

February 22, 1851. In conference met. Resolved that Brother Robert Boatman receive three dollars for keeping the house instead of $1.50 which was agreed to in December last. Adjourned. Owings, Mod. J. Greer, C. C.

March, 1851. Nothing done.

April 26, 1851. Nothing done. J. Greer, C. C. Owings, Mod.

May Sunday 25, 1851. Received by experience a collored man Ralph Rice also dismissed a colored man Anthony (Means). Also agreed to have a first Sunday meeting in June for the black people. J. Greer, C. C. Owings, Mod.

June 21, 1851. In conference met. First: a charge was preferred against Brother William Murphy for intoxication and appointed Brethren H. B. Murphy and Robert Boatman a committee to cite him to attend our next meeting to answer to said charges. J. Greer, C. C. Owings, Mod.

Sunday 22 Received on confession of faith Wyatt (Gist) a colored man.

July 2, 1851. In conference met. First: received by letter Franklin Rogers. Second: Brother William B. Murphy came forward and made acknowledgement which was received and he was restored. Third: Delegated Brethren J. Greer, I. P. Murphy and J. Gibbs to Bethel Association and J. L. Norman their alternate-- also appointed J. Greer to prepare a letter for the association. Adjourned J. Greer, C. C. Owings, Mod.

August 22, 1851. In conference met. First: agreed to send $7.00 to the association mission. Second: on motion it was resolved that Brother W. B. Murphy be excluded from the church for Habitual drunkness, and also excluded Brother George Nance for fighting and swearing. Fourth: A charge was brought against Brother Thomas Hart for Rolling Ten Pins at Union Court House, and appointed Brother J. Gibbs to cite him to attend out next meeting. Owings, Mod.

Sunday 23, in conference met. First: read and adopted the church letter. Second: Collected the sum of $2.00 for general purposes. J. Greer, C.C. Owings, Mod.

August 25, 1851. Collected $6.50 association missions.

August 26, 1851. Granted license to Brother John Gibbs to preach.

September 26, 1851. In conference met. Granted a letter of dismission to Sister Milly Lawson (White). Second: postponed the consideration of a letter from Mississippi in relation to a colored woman, Harriet. J. Greer, C. C. Parsley, Mod.

October 1851. In conference met. First: Brother Thomas Hart came forward and acknowledged that he was guilty of rolling ten pins for amusement, but desired the church to forgive him and that he would refrain from doing so in the future. He was accordingly forgiven. Second: agreed that our clerk answer a letter from Louisville, Miss. in relation to Harriet (Gage) case. Third: unanimously called Elder J. L. Norman to supply this church the ensuing year. J. Greer, Owings, Mod.

November 22, 1851. In conference met. First: Agreed to take up a subscription for the benefit of our supply Elder M. C. Owings. Adjourned J. Greer, C. C. Owings, Mod.

November 23, 1851. Restored Adam (Gist).

December 27, 1851. In conference met. First: Granted a letter of dismission to Prince (colored Man). Second: Took up a collection for general purposes of $3.15 cents. Third. Paid Brother Boatman three dollars for keeping the house and employed him for the next year for the same--say three dollars.

December 28, 1851. In conference. First: restored Charles (Gibbs). J. Greer, C. C. Owings, Mod.

January 24, 1852. In conference met. Received a request for help to ordain deacons from the Upper Fairforest Church. Request was granted and Brethren Norman and Vaughan was requested as the deacons of this church. Adjourned. J. Greer, J. L. Norman, Mod.

MINUTES OF LOWER FAIRFOREST BAPTIST CHURCH

February 21, 1852. In conference met. First: resolve that we the members of the Lower Fairforest Church in token of our high esteem for the faithful and Christian manner in which Elder M. C. Owings has labored amongst us as supply for the last four years; that each member extend to him the right hand of fellowship. Second: Resolve that we earnestly request Bro. Owings to attend us as often as convenient in future and especially for the next twelve months, as we feel that our young Brother J. L. Norman our present supply would feel much assisted in the arduous duties of his office. J. Hay, C. C. Protem. Norman, Mod.

March 27, 1852. In conference met. First agreed that out communion meetings be in April and August, the meeting in April commencing on Saturday. Second: Agreed to take up and answer the recommendation of the associational committee in relation to a correspondence or union of the Bethel and Salem association and in pursuance of which we have appointed Brothern I. P. Murphy, J. L. Norman a committee to prepare an instrument for the consideration of the church in June. Adjourned. J. Greer, C. C. Norman, Mod.

April 25, 1852. In conference met. First: collected the sum of one dollar and 75 cents for general purposes.

May 22, 1852. In conference met. First: a charge was preferred against Brother Thomas Hart for rolling ten pins and Brother Franklin Rogers nominated to cite him to attend our next meeting. Adjourned, J. Greer, C. C. Norman, Mod.

June 26, 1852. In conference met. First: Granted a letter of dismission to Nathan (Askew). Second: Received the report and discharged the committee. Third: adopted the report of the committee and ordained it to be engrossed with the association letter. Fourth: Took up the case of Brother Hart and after considerable discussion agreed to wait with him till next meeting. Fifth: resolve that this church desires singing at this place every fourth Sunday morning and that Bro. Norman be requested to procure the services of a competent teacher. J. Greer, C. C. Adjourned. Owings, Mod.

July 24, 1852. In conference met. First: Took up the cause of Br. Hart, he being present acknowledged the charges of rolling ten pins and desired the church to forgive him and also acknowledged that he had continued the same cause consequently he was excluded. Second: Delegated Elder J. L. Norman and Brothers J. Greer and I. P. Murphy, and in case of failure Elder C. C. Vaughan and J. Gibbs and appointed Brother J. Greer to prepare a letter. J. Greer, C. C. Adjourned. Norman, Mod.

August 20, 1852. In conference met. First: Read and adopted the church letter. Adjourned. J. Greer, C. C. Norman, Mod.

October 3, 1852. In conference met. First: collected the sum of one dollar and 95 cents for general purposes. J. Greer, C. C. Adjourned. Norman, Mod.

November 27, 1852. In conference met. First: Unanimously called Elder J. L. Norman to supply this church the ensuing year. Second: Took up a subscription for Brother Norman for his last year's services. Third: Excluded Jim (Murphy) for selling spirits, for which he was punished according to law. Adjourned. J. Greer, C. C.   J. Hay, Mod.

December 23, 1852. H. B. Murphy send 20 cents for general purposes.

January 22, 1853. In conference met. First: Elder J. L. Norman being present accepted the call of the church. Second: Granted a letter of dismission to Eliza (Murphy). Third: Employed Br. Boatman to keep the house for this year at $3.00. Fourth: Collected the sum of 95 cents for general purposes. J. Greer, C. C. Adjourned. Norman., Mod.

January 23, 1853. Paid Robert Boatman for keeping the house $3.00.

February 26, 1853. In conference met. Received from Sister T. Lawson 50 cents. J. Greer, C. C. Adjourned. Norman., Mod.

Sunday 27, 1853. In conference met. Adams (Nolon) came forward and acknowledged himself to be in great error, and desired the church to forgive him which was accordingly done. Second: excluded Julia (Murphy) for repeated dancing. Third: Granted a letter of dismission to Edmund (Rice). J. Greer, C. C.   Gibbs, Mod.

March 1853.

April 23, 1853. In conference met. First: Granted a letter of dismission to a colored man Ralph (Rice). Second: Received a letter from Sister Charlotte Murphy requesting her name to be stricken from the church book, the report was not granted, but appointed Br. I. P. Murphy and J. W. Murphy to wait on her, and to say that the church cannot grant her request for the reasons gave. Collected the sum of one dollar and 35 cents for general purposes. J. Greer, C. C. Adjourned.   Norman, Mod.

Sunday 24, 1853. Received by experience Judy (Noland).

May 21, 1853. In conference met. First: received by experience Marie (Noland).

June 1853.

July 21, 1853. In conference met. First: delegated Brother J. Greer, J. Gibbs, and I. P. Murphy to the Bethel Association and in case of failure J. L. Norman to prepare a letter, and also agreed to send two dollars and 50 cents for minutes. Second: Invited Elders Kindrick, Ezell, Felder, Barnett, R. Woodruff, and E. Rogers, and others to attend our protracted meeting to commence Friday before the 4th Sunday in August next. On motion adjourned. J. Greer, C.C. Vaughan, Mod.

August 26, 1853. In conference met. First: read and adopted the association letter. Second: Collected the sum of two dollars and 60 cents for general purposes. J. Greer, C. C. James Hay, Mod.

September, 1853. No meeting in consequence of the Association.

October 22, 1853. In conference met. First: Granted letters of dismission to Brother Hiram B. Murphy and sister Elizabeth Murphy, his wife and sister Juliana Murphy. Also Brother Robert Boatman and sister Deliah Boatman, his wife. Second: Brother C. Gibbs came forward and stated that he had been far out of the way by getting in a great passion and using hard and unbecoming language with a disposition to fight, and asked the church to forgive him, which was accordingly done. Third: Unanimously called Elder Drury Scruggs to supply this church for the ensuing year. Fourth: Agreed to pay brother Robert Boatman two dollars and 50 cents for keeping the house ten months. Fifth: Collected the sum of two dollars. J. Greer, C. C. Adjourned. J. Gibbs, Mod.

November 26, 1853. In conference met. First: Resolved that the keeping of the house be given to Brother John Gibbs in the same way and for the same compensation as was received by Brother Boatman, $3.00. J. Greer, C. C. Adjourned. Norman, Mod.

January 7, 1854. No meeting.

February 25, 1854. In conference met. First: Granted a letter of dismission to Rev. John L. Norman. J. Greer, C. C. Adjourned. Scruggs, Mod.

March 25, 1854. In conference met. Nothing done.

April 22, 1854. In conference met. 1st: agreed to take into prayerful consideration the subject of appointing a Deacon in place of Brother H. B. Murphy removed at our next meeting. J. Greer, Clk. Adjourned. D. Scruggs, Mod.

May 27, 1854. In conference met. First: Took up the subject of making a Deacon, but on motion it was postponed till our next meeting. Second: Resolved that we have protracted meeting commencing Friday before the fourth Sunday in July, and that Elders Norman, Ezell, Woodruff, Kindrick, Mullinax, T. D. Guinn, Mims, Barnett, and T. K. Presley be requested to attend the same. Third: Appointed Brother G. Harlin to request Brother F. Rogers to attend our next Meeting as the church desires to know his reasons for his non attendance at conference. J. Greer, C.C. Adjourned. Scruggs, Mod.

June 24, 1854. In conference met. First: Brother Harlin states that he saw Brother Rogers who acknowledged that he had been far out of the way, and intended to come to the church, but failed to attend, therefore, it was agreed to wait on him till at our next. Second: Proceeded to ballot for a deacon, the lot falling on Br. James Hay who consented to serve the church in that capacity. Also elected Brother J. W. Murphy singing clerk. J. Greer, C. C. Adjourned. Scruggs, Mod.

July 21, 1854. In conference met. First : A coloured Brother Jessey (Sparks) came forward and acknowledged that he had drunk too much spirits, but desired the church to forgive him, which was accordingly done, he promised to never drink again. Second: Took up the cause of Brother Rogers, but he not being present, and nothing being heard from him, it was again suspended. Third: Delegated Brother I. P. Murphy, J. Greer, and J. Gibbs and in case of failure Brother C. C. Vaughan and James Hay to the Bethel Association and requested Brother J. Greer to prepare a letter for the same. Also agreed to send $2.50 for minutes. Fourth: Jim (Murphy) came forward and desired the church to restore him, but the church declined to do so. J. Greer, C. C. Adjourned. Gibbs., Mod.

Saturday 22. [no minutes]

Sunday 23, 1854. [no minutes]

July 24, 1854. Dismissed Wyatt and Delphy (Colored).

_____ 25. Ordained Brother James Hay and set him apart for the office of a deacon.

_____26. Received by experience Dicey Hay. Our protracted meeting closed.

August 26, 1854. In conference met. First: A charge was made against Br. Rogers for swearing, gaming and other misconduct receiving at same time a letter from him requesting his name to be taken from the church book. In consideration of which he was excluded. Second: Read and adopted the association letter. Third: Resolved that a committee consisting of the deacons and the clerk of this church be appointed to identify the land belonging to this church and to endeavor to obtain a deed to such other lands as may be considered necessary for the church and graveyard. Fourth: Collected the sum of two dollars and 35 cents for general purposes. J. Greer, C. C. Adjourned. D. Scruggs, Mod.

September, 1854. No meeting

October 21, 1854. In conference met. First: Received by experience a colored woman Rachel (McBeth) also restored Jim (Murphy). Second: Granted a letter of dismission to Jacob (McBeth). Third: Unanimously called Elder D.

Scruggs to supply the church the next year. J. Greer, C. C. Adjourned. D. Scruggs, Mod.

October 24, 1854. Received by experience Mary Gibbs.

November 25, 1854. In conference met. First: Restored a colored man Jesse (Whitmire). Second: the committee appointed to identify the lands of the church reported that they had accomplished the work assigned them, consequently they were discharged. Third: Keeping of the house was given to Bro. James Hay in place of Br. J. Gibbs for the same compensation say $3.00. Fourth: Elder D. Scruggs agreed to serve the church the next year. J. Greer, Ck. Adjourned. D. Scruggs, Mod.

December 23, 1854. In conference met. First Collected for General purposes $3.00. Second: Paid an act of Br. James Hay for repairs of window, 25 cents. J. Greer, Ck. Adjourned. D. Scruggs, Mod.

January 27, 1855. In conference met. First: Br. C. Gibbs came forward and acknowledged that he had been far out of the way by intoxication but craved the forgiveness of the church which was accordingly done and he was restored to fellowship. J. Greer, Ck. Adjourned. D. Scruggs, Mod.

February 24, 1855. In conference met. Nothing done. J. Greer. Ck Adjourned Scruggs, Mod.

March 1855. In conference met, nothing done. J. Greer, Ck. Adjourned. D. Scruggs, Mod.

April 21, 1855. In conference met. First: Postponed our communion season till our next. J. Greer, Ck. Adjourned. J. Gibbs, Mod.

Sunday 22, 1855. Dismissed a coloured sister Liller (Askew).

May 26, 1855. In conference. First: postponed our communion till August. On motion adjourned. J. Greer, Ck. Scruggs, Mod.

June 23, 1855. In conference met. First: appointed John Gibbs, James Hay and I. P. Murphy a committee to report to our next what they conceived to be a proper expression of the church, in relation to a reunion of the Bethel and Salem Associations.

Sunday 24, 1855. Received by letter a coloured woman, Hannah (Gibbs). Also received a letter from Rev. G. C. Grimes tending his services to this church at our protracted meeting. James Hay, Ck. protem. D. Scruggs, Mod.

July 21, 1855. In conference met. First: Received and adopted the report of the committee on the reunion of the two associations. Second: Appointed Br. Greer to answer a letter of Rev. G. C. Grimes tending a special invitation to attend our protracted meeting commencing on Friday before the 4th Sunday in August next. Third: Delegated Brother I. P. Murphy. J. Greer, James Hay to the Bethel Association and J. W. Murphy in case of failure. J. Greer to prepare a letter for the association, also agreed to send $2.50 for minutes. J. Greer, Ck. Adjourned. D Scruggs. Yod.

August 25, 1855. In conference met. First: Adopted the church letter. Second: postponed the communion till at our next.

August 28. Received by experience Sister Nancy Lawson.

August 29. Received by experience Sister Mary Jane Greer.

September, 1855. No conference. Association

October, 1855. In conference met. First: Unanimously called Elder D. Scruggs to supply this church the ensuing year. J. Greer, Ck. Adjourned D. Scruggs. Mod.

November, 1855. In conference met. First: Unanimously called Elder J. G. Kindrick to supply this church the ensuing year. Second: Excluded Wyatt (Gist) for disorderly conduct. Third: Granted a letter of dismission to Jesse (Whitmire). J. Greer, Ck. Adjourned. D. Scruggs, Mod.

December 1855. No meeting.

January 1856. No meeting in consequence of bad weather.

February 1856. Brother Kendrick being present agreed to comply with the wishes of the church. J. Greer, Ck. Adjourned. Kendrick, Mod.

March 22, 1856. In conference met. First: Took up a collection for church purposes, amounting to $4.50. On motion paid Brother James Hay for the care of the meeting house, $3.00. Second: Agreed to let the keeping of the house to Brother J. Gibbs till the end of the year which he agreed to do gratuously. J. Greer, Ck. Adjourned. Kendrick, Mod.

April 26, 1856. In conference met. First: Appointed Elder C. Felder to preach a missionary sermon at this church on the ----. J. Greer, Ck. Adjourned. Kendrick, Mod.

May 24, 1856. In conference met. First: delegated C. C. Vaughan, J. Gibbs and I. P. Murphy, J. Greer, and James Hay to the convention to be held at Cool Branch Church said delegates to draft a letter to said convention to be approved or disapproved by this church. Resolve that this church hold a protracted meeting, commencing Saturday before the 4th Sabbath in July and that Bro. I. P. Murphy be instructed to write to Bro. Scruggs and Barnet to attend the same. James Hay, Ck. Protem. Adjourned. Kendrick, Mod.

June 2, 1856. In conference met. First: Received and adopted the report of the committee on the convention letter viz: Resolved that we address our letter to the delegates of the Bethel Association that may be assembled in convention at Cool Branch Church Friday before the 2nd Sabbath in August 1856. Resolve also that the following resolutions be drafted in our letter Viz: Resolve that the church, so far as she is concerned with associations retain the name, constitution and order of the Bethel Association. Second: Br. Greer to write the said convention. Third: Changed our protracted meeting to Saturday before the 4th Sabbath in August. J. Greer., Ck. Adjourned. Kendrick, Mod.

July 26, 1856. In conference met. First: received and adopted the letter to the convention. Second: Delegated Brethren I. P. Murphy, J. Greer, and James Hay to the Bethel Association and J. W. Murphy and J. C. Bobo alternates also requested Br. Greer to prepare a letter for said association. J. Greer, Ck. Adjourned. Kendrick, Mod.

August 23, 1856. In conference met. First: received the report of our delegates to the convention. Second: Read and adopted the associational letter. Third: Resolved that we invite the Bethel Association to hold its next meeting with us. Fourth: Collected for minutes $.2.85 cents also postponed the communion till our meeting in October. J. Greer, Ck. Adjourned. Kendrick, Mod.

August 28, 1856. Received the following persons by experience. Unity Lawson, Peggy Lawson, Lucinda Tucker, Betsy Tucker, Nevil Howard, Jane Sanders, Elizabeth Sparks, Sarah Holcomb, Jane Greer.

August 29, 1856. Restored Julia (Murphy).

September, 1856. No conference

October 25, 1856. Granted letters of dismission to Br. Nevil G. Howard, and Sister Eleanor Comer. Second: appointed James Hay, John Gibbs and H. G. Holcomb, a committee to superintend the building of the Brick Pool and dressing house. Third: C. Gibbs came forward and acknowledged himself to have been far out of the way in being provoked Into a violent passion and saying harsh words, after considerable discussion on the subject it was agreed that the subject be postponed till the next conference. Fourth: unanimously called Elder J. G. Kendrick to supply the church the next year. J. Greer, Ck. Adjourned. Kendrick, Mod.

November 22, 1856. In conference met. First: resolved that Brethren J. W. Murphy and G. Harlan headed to the committee on building the brick pool and that Brother J. Gibbs be discharged from the said committee. Second: Took up the cause of Br. C. Gibbs he not being present. it was agreed to postpone, till at our next meeting. J. Greer, Ck. Adjourned. Gibbs., Mod.

MINUTES OF LOWER FAIRFOREST BAPTIST CHURCH

December 27, 1856. In conference met. First: Took up the case of Br. C. Gibbs he being present proceeded to give the church entire satisfaction and was restored to fellowship. Second: Collected two dollars and 85 cents for general purposes. J. Greer, Ck. Adjourned. Gibbs, Mod.

January 24, 1857. In conference met. First: Unanimously called Elder C. C. Vaughan to the supply of the church. Elder Kendrick declined to serve. J. Greer, Ck. Adjourned. W. Gordon., Mod.

February 21. 1857. In conference met. First: Elder C. C. Vaughan being present agreed to consent to serve the church the present year. J. Greer, Ck. Adjourned. Vaughan, Mod.

March 22, 1857. In conference met. First: received by experience Byram Sparks. Second: Dismissed Sister Jane Gibbs. J. Greer, Ck. Adjourned. Vaughan, Mod.

April 1857. In conference met. First: received by experience Kazia (McBeth) also dismissed Lotty Palmer by letter. James Hay, Ck. Protem. Vaughan, Mod.

May 23, 1857. In conference. First: received by experience Lucy (McBeth). J. Greer, Ck. Adjourned. S. Drummond, Mod.

May 24, 1857. Received by experience negroes Tom (Noland), Bill (Norris), Judy (Gee) and Independence (McBeth).

June 27, 1857. In conference met. First: received by letter Br. James W. Jones. Second: Appointed a protracted meeting to commence at this place embracing the fourth Sabbath in August next. J. Greer, Ck. Adjourned. Vaughan, Mod.

July 25, 1857. In conference met. First: delegated Br. I. P. Murphy J. Greer, and James Hay to the Bethel Association, and J. W. Murphy their alternate. Br. Greer to write also agreed to send $2.50 for minutes. J. Greer, Ck. Adjourned. Gibbs, Mod.

August 22, 1857. In conference met. First: Collected for minutes $2.85. J. Greer, Ck. Adjourned. Vaughan, Mod.

August 24, 1857. In conference. First: Restored Susan Sparks to fellowship.

September, 1857. No meeting.

October, 1857. First: received by experience, Martha (McBeth). Second: Granted letters of dismission to Br. James Hay and wife, also to Alsey (Gist). Adjourned.

November 21, 1857. In conference. First: Granted letters of dismission to Brother John Hay and wife Dicey Hay, and Sister Sarah Holcomb also to

Willis, Jenny, Dicey, and Sam colored of (Mr. Prince). Second: Unanimously called Elder C. C. Vaughan to supply this Church the ensuing year. Third: appointed a committee of Br. John Gibbs, I. P. Murphy and George Harlin to suggest a plan of improvement to this house and to report said plan with the probable cost at our next meeting. J. Greer, Ck. Adjourned. Vaughan, Mod.

December 26, 1857. In conference met. First: Unanimously called Elder S. Head to supply this church. J. Greer, Ck. Adjourned. Gibbs, Mod.

December 27, 1857. Granted letters of dismission to Elder C. C. Vaughan and Br. John Gibbs. also received by experience Caroline. (McBeth). J. Greer, Ck.

May 8, 1858. In conference met. Appointed Br. George Harlin to wait on Jim Murphy and report at our next. Second: the church agreed to inquire after old Abram and if proper to grant him a letter. J. C. Bobo, Ck. Protem.

June [no minutes]

July [no minutes]

August 7, 1858. In conference. First: excluded Jim (Murphy) for drunkness. Second: Granted letters of dismission to sister Lucinda Tucker, and Elizabeth Hart. Third: Delegated I. P. Murphy, J. Greer, and J. C. Bobo to meet the Bethel Association and J. Greer to prepare a letter for the same. Communion in September. J. Greer, Ck. Adjourned. Seymour, Mod.

September, 1858. In conference met. First: Received by letters Nancy and Frances McCright. Second: Read and adopted the association letter. J. Greer, Ck. Adjourned. Gibbs, Mod.

October 28, 1858. Received by experience William J. Sparks, also baptised two coloured persons.

October 29, 1858. In conference met. First: granted a letter of dismission to Sister Mary McCreight. Second: Unanimously called Elder Julius White to supply this church the ensuing year, and appointed Brother J. W. Murphy to bear our message to him. J. Greer, Ck. I. P. Murphy, Mod.

November 27, 1858. In conference met. First: Elder J. White being present consented to serve the church the ensuing year. J. Greer, Ck. Adjourned. J. White, Mod.

December, 1858.

January, 1859.

MINUTES OF LOWER FAIRFOREST BAPTIST CHURCH

February, 1859.

March 26, 1859. In conference met. Nothing done.

March 27, 1859. Received by letter a colored man Africa (Keenan).

April 23, 1859. In conference nothing done.

April 24, 1859. Received by letter Nancy (Keenan)

May 1859. Nothing done.

June 25, 1859. In conference met. First: appointed the next meeting of this church to be 9 o'clock a. m. on conference day in order to take into Consideration and form plans for the repairs of this church. Second: preferred charges against Tom and Lucy colored persons for living in disorder and appointed Br. W. J. Murphy, Sparks and J. Greer to summon them to attend at our next conference to answer.

July 23, 1859. First: Lucy colored appeared and gave the church satisfaction. Second: Delegated Br. J. Greer, William J. Sparks and J. C. Bobo to the Bethel Association and also Byrum Sparks and in case of failure appointed Br. J. Greer, to prepare a letter to the same. J. Greer, Ck. Adjourned. White, Mod.

August 27, 1859. In conference. First: received by letter Sister Elizabeth Robinson. Second: received and adopted the report of the committee on repairing the house. Third: Read and adopted the associational letter. Fourth: Collected the sum of $1.40. Fifth: Resolve that J. Gibbs, J. Greer, and any and all the neighbors that see proper to assist, are at liberty to build a school house on the church land and to have the full privilege of using it as a school house as long, as the neighborhood sees proper to do so provided they permit the church to use it on all occasions when the school is not in session. J. Greer, ck. Adjourned. White, Mod.

Sunday, August 28, 1859. First: Received by letter George and Mary colored (Keenan). Second: Tom (Noland) cause was brought up and he was acquitted. Third: Granted letters of dismission to William Prince and Judy colored (Norris) and Kesiah.

September 24. 1859. In conference. First: received by experience Sarah Ann Barnett.

October, 1859. In conference. First: Agreed that at our next meeting we make a selection of a minister to supply the church the ensuing year.

November, 1859. In conference met. Nothing done.

December 24, 1859. In conference met. made a call it resulted in choice Julius White who agreed to serve.

January 1860. In conference met. Nothing worth recording done. J. Gibbs, Ck. White, Mod.

February, 1860. In conference met. Nothing worth recording done. J. C. Bobo, Ck. White, Mod.

March 24, 1860. In conference. First: It was moved and seconded that Br. J. C. Bobo be authorized to act as clerk protem, until we learn whether or not brother J. Greer will resume the office with us as clerk again from his disease and that Bro. Bobo be authorized to get of Brother Greer the church book, Second. Brother C. Gibbs report that he had received on a subscription list to aid in repairing this house Twenty four dollars and that he had paid twenty one dollars and fifteen cents for shingles for the same purpose (i. e.) for repairing, leaving the balance on what he had collected of two dollars and eighty five cents, which balance the church decided to vote to give brother ____ for hauling and other service rendered toward the improvement of this house. Third: Brother Bobo moved that there be a committee of three be appointed to superintend the repairing and they be authorized to sell the brick of the gable ends, Which are to be taken down and that this committee be empowered to make some suitable contract with some person or persons to do the work, This was voted upon and was unanimously carried, the committee is to consist of Brethren J. Bobo, G. Harlin, and B. Sparks. Fourth: It was moved and seconded that we elect two deacons for the use of this church by balloting. It resulted in the choice of Brethren W. J. Sparks and J. C. Bobo who agreed to serve to the best of their ability. Fifth: It was moved and seconded that the ordination of the brethren as deacons be Postponed until our July meeting, which is to be protracted according to circumstances. Sixth: The church was then dismissed. J. W. Jones, Ck. for the day. White, Mod.

April 22d, 1860. Sunday. In conference met. 1st: Moved that an inquiry be made for the nonattendance of our two sisters Elizabeth Robertsons (both the same name). Brother J. W. Murphy and wife, Sister Mary Ellis, that Brother G. Harlin inquire of the Sister Robertsons and Sister Ellis. And that Brother I. P. Murphy inquire of Brother J. W. Murphy and wife. 2d: Appointed Brother J. C. Bobo our regular recording clerk and brother J. Jones regular Treasurer. 3rd: Moved that Brothren W. J. Sparks and J. C. Bobo be authorized to get and examine the Treasurer's book and report next meeting. J. C. Bobo, Ck. White, Mod.

May 26, 1860. In conference met. 1st: received the report of Br. G. Harland he said the sisters, Robertsons and Sister Ellis were so cituated as not to make it convenient to attend regular, they craved the indulgence of the church, they were unanimously excused. 2nd: Received the report of Br. I. P. Murphy and said that Brother J. W. Murphy being present said that his nonattendance was created by the removal on dismissal and the ordination of Brother John Gibbs.

3rd: Moved and passed his case be postponed until our next meeting and that brother J. Gibbs be requested to attend. 4th: The examination of the Treasurer's book was postponed until our next, the committee not being ready to report. 5th: A motion to adjourn was carried. J. C. Bobo, Ck. White, Mod.

June 23, 1860. In conference met. First: Took up the case of Brother J. W. Murphy he said that his mind had not changed since our last meeting and after much discussion, the case was postponed until our next conference. Second: It was moved and passed that our next meeting conference on Friday and conference be held that day. Third: It was again moved that our supply and our brother clerk be authorized to invite ministerial aid at our next meeting to assist in the setting apart of two brethren to the office of deacon and also to assist in retracting the meeting. Fourth: Received the report of the committee our treasurer acting. Reported the church $1.92 due the treasurer. Report received and the committee discharged. Fifth: Read the records and adjourned. J. C. Bobo, Ck. White, Mod.

July 1860. In conference met. First: granted a letter of dismission to James W. Jones. Second: Received a request from the Calvery Church asking a letter of dismission for a colored woman named Delphy. It was agreed that her case be postponed and search be made for her character until our next meeting conference. Third: Took up the case of Br. J. W. Murphy and after some discussion it was again postponed until our next meeting for the purpose of the church laboring together privately concerning his case. Fourth: Delegated to the Bethel Association our Brethren J. C. Bobo, George Harland, I. P. Murphy and as alternate W. J. Sparks and Churchill Gibbs to represent us at its session. Fifth: That our clerk address a letter to the said association.

July 21, 1860. The church proceeded, as before resolved to set apart the two candidates to the office of deacon. The introductory sermon was delivered by Elder J. White and after which the Presbytery was organized of the following Brethren viz: ministers from

New Prospect	Elder John Gibbs
Corrinth	Elder William F. Lee
Philadelphia	Elder J. C. White (supply)
Liberty	Elder G. W. Picket

Deacons:
Union Church	James Lancaster
	Cipryan Pruette

The church then presented the candidates and being examined in due form after that they were then set apart according to the prescription of the Bible: and then received a solemn charged; the ordination was then considered complete.

July 24, 1860. Received by experience Nancy Greer. J. C. Bobo, Ck. White, Mod.

August 25, 1860. In conference met. First: Granted a letter dismission to sister Mary Ellis. Second: That the clerk be authorized to answer the request of the Cavalry church to the best of information he can get from the records concerning a colored sister (Delphy). Third: Took up the case of Br. J. W. Murphy and after some discussion of his case and he remaining in the same mind as before. Fourth: There was then a charge preferred against him for obstinacy and contempt of authority. Then after further discussion the church excluded him from her fellowship, his wife (Sister Nancy Murphy) requested her name erased, but after discussion her case was postponed indefinitely.

August 27, 1860. In conference met. First: Baptized sister Nancy Greer. Second: Read and adopted the associational letter. Third: Agreed to send two dollars and fifty cents for printing minutes. Fourth: appointed Bro. J. C. Bobo our regular treasurer. I. C. Bobo, C. C. White, Mod.

September 22, 1860. No meeting on account of the association. J. C. Bobo, Ck. White, Mod.

October 27, 1860. In conference met. First: Bro. C. Gibbs came forward and said that he had been out of the way by being in a difficulty and begged to be excused, the church then acquitted him. Second: called the case of sister Nancy Murphy. She not being present her case was continued. Third: The church then selected a supply In the choice of Elder Richard Woodruff who being present on the Sabbath consented to serve. Fourth: Also liberated our present supply and requested him to attend our meeting in December Next. J. C. Bobo, Ck. I. White, Mod.

November 24, 1860. No meeting in consequence of the bad weather.

December 22, 1860. In conference met. First: posponed the collection for general purposes until our next meeting. J. C. Bobo, Ck. J. Gibbs, Mod.

January 26, 1861. In conference met. No meeting on the occasion of bad weather. J. C. Bobo.

February 24, 1861. Sunday, In conference met. First: Received by letter Elder W. F. Lee and his wife Malissia Lee. Second: Dismissed Sisters Nancy and Frances McCreight by letter. J. C. Bobo, Ck. R. Woodruff, Mod.

March 23, 1861. In conference met. Nothing done. J. C. Bobo, Ck. R. Woodruff, Mod.

MINUTES OF LOWER FAIRFOREST BAPTIST CHURCH

April 27, 1861. In conference met. Elder W. F. Lee sung and offered prayer adjourned. J. C. Bobo, Ck. W. F. Lee, Mod.

May 25, 1861. In conference met. First: the church then made a call to supply the church during Brother Woodruff's absence which resulted In the choice of Br. W. F. Lee. Second: The Bro. Clerk to take the overplus of money that was contributed to the repair of the house; and pay all dues of the church and procure a lock for the door if enough money. W. F. Lee, Ck. Protem J. Gibbs, Mod.

June 22, 1861. In conference met. First: That our meeting in August be protracted according to circumstances and that Brethren Lee and Gibbs are authorized to invite ministerial aid.

Resolutions: Resolve First that we recommend to all Denominations throughout the Confederate States, the propriety of holding a prayer meeting, the space of one hour; say from 10 O'clock to 11 a. m. on their respective meeting days every Sabbath to the God of all battles, for our delivery from our insidious enemies. Second: Resolve that we solicit the publication of this throughout the entire South. J. C. Bobo, Ck., W. F. Lee

July 26, 1861. In conference met. First: Cited Brother C. Gibbs to attend our next Conference to answer to a charge of using Profane language and fighting also appointed brother W. F. Lee and George Harland to wait on him. Second: Took up the case of sister Nancy Murphy and postponed until our next. Appointed Brother J. C. Bobo to cite her to attend or to know her cause for not attending regular. Third: Delegated Brethren J. C. Bobo, George Harland, W. J. Sparks and as alternate B. Sparks to represent us at the next session of the Bethel Association. Appointed our clerk to prepare an associational letter. Fifth: Agreed to send one dollar and fifty cents for printing the minutes of the association. J. C. Bobo Ck. Adjourned. W. F. Lee, Mod.

August 24, 1861. In conference met. First: Took up the case of Br. C. Gibbs, after some discussion, the case was postponed till our next conference. Second: Took up the case of Sister Nancy Murphy after discussing of her case there was a charge prefered against her for obstinacy and a contempt of authority after further discussion of the case the church then excluded her from its fellowship. Third: Received and adopted the associational letter with the clerk to have authority to amend so as to include our support of our Sabbath school and other intelligence. Fourth: That we set a part the Saturday before the second Sabbath in September to repare the fencing of our graveyard. Fifth: That our next conference be on the fifth or include the same Sabbath in September on the account of the association.

August 25. Meeting continued

August 26. Meeting continued with much interest.

August 27. Meeting continued and received William Willard by experience.

August 28. Meeting continued and received Anna Willard by experience.
J. C. Bobo, Ck. Lee, Mod.

September 28, 1861. In conference met. First. Took up the case of Br. C. Gibbs, It was then postponed until its termination by law. Second: That he has no voice with the church until his case is settled by laws. J. C. Bobo, Ck. Lee, Mod.

October, 1861. Received by letter sister Ellen Gibbs.

November, 1861. No meeting.

December, 1861. No meeting.

January, 1862. No meeting.

February, 1862. Called Brother J. C. Carter to supply the church to which he consented. J. C. Bobo, Ck.

March 22, 1862. In conference met. First: received and adopted the report of the committee on repairs of the meeting house; all the business not being settled up, the committee was not discharged. J. Bobo, Clk. Carter, Mod.

April, 1862. No minutes.

May 24, 1862. In conference met. Nothing done. J. C. Bobo, Ck.
Carter, Mod.

June 8, 1862. Church met and sent a request to Unity Church to set apart Bro. J. C. Carter to the office of the ministry of Gospel. J. C. Bobo, Ck. W. F. Lee, Mod

June 21, 1862. In conference met. First: Unanimously elected Bro. George Harland to serve as Deacon of the church. Second: That at our next meeting be set apart to the office as Deacon and our meeting to be protracted according to circumstances. Third: Appointed Thursday and Friday before our next meeting to repair the Graveyard fencing. J.C. Bobo, Ck. J. G. Carter, Mod.

July 26, 1862. In conference met. First: received sister Lucinda Tucker by letter. Second: Elected Brethren J. C. Bobo and George Harland, I. P. Murphy and in case of alternate W. J. Sparks to represent us in the next session of the association; Appointed Br. J. C. Bobo to prepare a letter to the same. Third: Agreed to send $1.50 for the printing of the Associational minutes. Fourth: That we invite the next meeting of the Association to hold it next session with us.

MINUTES OF LOWER FAIRFOREST BAPTIST CHURCH

July 27, 1862. Sunday. The church proceeded to the ordination of Bro. George Harland after organizing the undersigned presbytery.

Minister:	Congaree Church	Elder W. D. Beverly
	Pacolet Church	Elder J. G. Kendrick
	New Prospect	Elder J. Gibbs

Deacons:

| | New Prospect | Jesse Sparks |
| | Padgetts Creek | W. W. Bobo and W. M. Roberson |

With the deaconship of the church, W. J. Sparks, J. C. Bobo.
J. C. Bobo, Sec.   W. D. Beverly, Chairman

July 28, 1862. Meeting continued with great zeal and effect with many mourners.

July 29. Continued with the same effect.

July 30. Received on experience Martha Sanders, Amanda Roberson, Martha Sparks.

July 31. Received by experience Ann Parks and Emily Barnett. Agreed to minister the ordinance of Baptism the next meeting.
J. C. Bobo, Ck.   I. G. Carter., Mod.

August 23, 1862. In conference met. After divine service by Bro. Carter, First: received by experience sister Anna Barnett. Second: Read and adopted the associational letter. Administered the ordinance of Baptism. J. C. Bobo, Ck. J. G. Carter, Mod.

September 25, 1862. No meeting on account of the association.

October 25, 1862. In conference met. After Divine services by Elder G. W. Phillips and J. Gibbs. First: received Amanda Sparks by experience. Second: Postponed the case of the defaulters, Bro. C. Gibbs, I. P. Murphy and sister Silvia R. Murphy until our next. Third: Postponed the call till our next meeting and that the church take up a collection for our pastor supply. J. C. Bobo, Ck.   J. G. Carter, Mod.

November 22, 1862. In conference met. After Divine Services by Elder J. G. Carter, First: Opened the doors of the church for the reception of members-- no one presented. Second: Invited brethren and sisters of other churches to seats with the church. Third: the case of Brother C. Gibbs who came forward and made acknowledgement of his case--which was received unanimously. Fourth: The church unanimously called Elder J. G. Carter to supply the church the ensuing year.
T. F. Murphy, Ck. Protem   J. G. Carter, Mod.

December 20, 1862. No conference.

January 24, 1863. No conference.

February 21, 1863. No conference.

March 21, 1863. No conference.

April 25 1863. In conference met. No business done.

May 23, 1863. In conference met. No business done.

June 27, 1863. After Divine Services by Elder F. Lee First: Appointed committee to investigate the report concerning Brother J. C. Bobo viz: W. T. Sparks, George Harland, and C. Gibbs who are to report at the next. J. C. Bobo, Ck.   J. G. Carter, Mod.

July 25, 1863. In conference met. After Divine Services by Elder J. Gibbs, and J. G. Carter. First: received by letter sister Laura Gibbs. Second: Called for the report of the committee appointed to investigate a report concerning Brother J. C. Bobo--report received but reported that met according to appointment and did not act but requested that the church would call for assistance from other sister churches. Third: That we call on our sister churches New Prospect and Union for them to send us three brethren each to act in conjunction with our committee in investigating the report concerning our brother J. C. Bobo and to settle the matter. Fourth: delegated our beloved Brethren George Harlan, Churchhill Gibbs, J. C. Bobo and as alternate W. J. Sparks to the Bethel Association and that the clerk prepare a letter to the same, and that we send five dollars for the printing of the minutes of the association.   J. C. Bobo, Ck.   J. G. Carter, Mod.

Called Meeting

August 14, 1863. In conference met. After Divine Services by Elder W. F. Lee-- First: Called the committee called for the report of the committee called on to investigate the report of Brother J. C. Bobo which report was received and adopted which reads as follows viz: We your committee leave to report that from a thorough examination of all the papers and evidence that we can arrive at; that we can not find brother J. C. Bobo guilty of the charge alledged to him. Ulyses Williams, Chairman.

Second: Read and adopted the associational letter. Third: Set apart Thursday preceeding the Third Sunday in September next to meet at this place to make preparations for the association and that we request the vicinity in general to assist us.

September, 1863. No meeting in consequence of the association.

MINUTES OF LOWER FAIRFOREST BAPTIST CHURCH

October, 1863. No conference in consequence of the bad weather.

November 22, 1863. Sunday in conference met. First: Moved to call a supply which resulted in the unanimous choice of Elder J. G. Carter. J. C. Bobo, C. C. Adjourned. R. M. Robinson, Mod.

December 26, 1863. No meeting in consequence of unfavorable weather.

January 23, 1864. In conference met. First: granted a letter of dismission to sister Ann Pruitt. Second: Called for the excuse of defaulters at conference meetings. When Brother C. Gibbs made the excuse for his wife which was granted--it being to attend to the Post office. Third: Read the rules of our faith and practice. Fourth: Motion was made requesting the next conference to transact business of importance returning to the rules of the church. J. C. Bobo, C. C. Adjourned. J. C. Carter, Mod.

February 24, 1864. In conference met. After Divine services by Elder J. C Carter. First: Postponed the case of defaulters until our next meeting. J. C. Bobo, C. C. J. G. Carter, Mod.

March 26, 1864. In conference met. After Divine Services by Elder J. G. Carter church met and no conference. J. C. Bobo, Ck. Adjourned. J. G. Carter, Mod.

April 23, 1864. In conference met after divine services by Elder J. G. Carter. First: Granted letters of dismission to Elder W. P. Lee and Sister Meliscia Lee his wife. Second: Again postponed the case of defaulters indefinitely. J. C. Bobo, Ck. Adjourned. J. G. Carter, Mod.

May 21, 1864. In church conference met after Divine Services by Elder J. C. Carter. First: Passed a resolution which reads as follows: Resolve that we as a church do give to those who have been nonattending to church conference to attend regularly--if not without providential hindrance the rules of the church will be enforced. J. C. Bobo, Ck. Adjourned. J. G. Carter, Mod.

June 26, 1864. In conference met. After Divine Services by Elder J. G. Carter. First: After reading the proceedings of last meeting Br. I. P. Murphy considering himself a defaulter came forward and expressed his cause of absence, Second: His case was then postponed until our next meeting for the purpose of the members consulting one with another concerning his case. Third: That Brethren W. J. Sparks and George Harland be appointed to summon Bro. William Willard and wife, Sister Holly Sparks, Martha Sparks, Susannah Sparks, and Sister Sarah A. Barnett (widow) to give their excuses for their nonattendance at conferences for some considerable length of time. J. C. Bobo, C. C. Adjourned. J. G. Carter, Mod.

July 23, 1864. In conference met after Divine services by Elder J. Carter and Gibbs. First: Received Brother Jesse J. Gwin by letter. Second: Took up the case of Brother I. P. Murphy moved that he be notified (he not being present) that if he does not comply with the rules of the church he will be excluded at our next meeting. Appointed Bro. J. C. Bobo to notify him and also to inquire of Sister Sylvia Murphy the reason of her nonattendance at church meetings. Third: Called for the report of the committee appointed last meeting, to inquire of those who have been nonattending, the report concerning Bro. W. Willard not satisfactory and he not being present his case was postponed till our next meeting. Sister Williard's report was satisfactory. She expressed a desire to be with the church but the distance was so great that she could not attend regularly. Sister Holly Sparks being present gave the church satisfaction and desired to continue with the church upon which she was excused for her absence. Sister Martha Sparks being present expressed a dissatisfaction with Bro. J. C. Bobo when her case was postponed until our next for them to settle the matter privately. Sister Susan Sparks not being present her case was postponed indefinitely. Sister Sarah A. Barnett not being present her case was postponed until December meeting. Fourth: Delegated Brethren G. Harland, Jesse J. Gwin, J. C. Bobo, to the Bethel Association as alternate Bro. W. J. Sparks. Appointed Bro. Bobo to prepare the letter to the same. Fifth: Appointed Bro. J. C. Bobo to write out a sketch of the life of Bro. John F. Sparks who died in the service of his country. Sixth: That it be published tomorrow that on our next meeting give the colored members an opportunity to have worship and for the church to inquire into their standing. J. C. Bobo, C. C. Adjourned. J. G. Carter, Mod.

August 27, 1864. In conference met. After Divine Services by J. G. Carter. First: Taken up the case of Bro. I. P. Murphy and after some discussion the church agreed to bear with him-- he expressing a willingness and a desire to continue a member. Second: Taken up the case of Sister Silvia Murphy after some reflections on her case the church agreed to bear with her as she has an inability to attend church meetings. Third: Taken up the case of Bro. William Willard and after some discussion and deliberations on his conduct and he promising to attend and did not, the church prepared a charge against him. Obstinacy and a contempt of authority then after some reflections he was excluded on the charge above named. Taken up the case of Sister Martha Sparks, posponed until our next conference. Fourth: Read and adopted the association letter. Collected the sum of twelve dollars for the printing of the minutes. Collected he sum of sixteen dollars for benevolent purposes.

August 28, 1864. Sunday. In conference for the blacks. First: Called over and corrected the list of names of the colored members and inquired into their standing. Second: Preferred a charge against Adam (Noland) for living in disorder--postponed until next meeting. Third: Preferred a charge against Martha (McBeth) for fornication posponed until next meeting. Fourth: Taken into consideration, the manner in which Tom (Noland) is living--postponed until next. J. C. Bobo, C. C. Adjourned. G. Carter, Mod.

September 23, 1864. No conference on account of association.

October 22, 1864. In conference met. After Divine Services by Elder J. G. Carter and W. F. Lee. First: Taken up the case of Sister Martha Sparks postponed until next meeting. Second: Taken up the case of Adam (Noland) the church excluded him for living in polygamy. Third: Taken up the case of Martha (McBeth) the church excluded her for fornication. Fourth: Taken up the case of Tom (Noland) postponed until next meeting. Fifth: Received a report from the proceedings of the Association. Sixth: Elder Lee stated that he had been out of the way by having a difficulty with a neighbor--he giving the church satisfaction was acquitted. Seventh: By his request his letter was recalled and a new one granted. Eighth: The church made a call for a supply for the next year which resulted in choice of Rev. W. D. Bevelly and that Bro. I. C. Bobo wait on him. J. C. Bobo, C. C. Adjourned. J. C. Carter, Mod.

November 26, 1864. In conference met. After prayer by Elder J. G. Carter, 1st: Taken up the case of Martha Sparks and after some consideration of her case the church excluded her for immoral conduct. 2nd: Taken up the case of Tom (Noland) and after some discussion the church agreed to bear with him. 3rd: The church went into a call to supply the church the ensuing year, Elder W. D. Beverly not being capacitated to attend the church, but granted him the privilege of preaching as often as his opportunities will permit. The call resulted in the unanimous choice of Elder Warren Drummond and nominated Bro. J. C. Bobo to inform him of the call. Fourth: the church resolved to support the home missionary cause. J. C. Bobo. Adjourned J. C. Carter, Mod.

December 24, 1864. No meeting on account of supply.

January 21, 1865. No meeting on account of unfavorable weather.

March 25, 1865. No conference.

April 22, 1865. No conference.

May 20, 1865. No conference.

June 24, 1865. No conference.

July 22, 1865. In conference met--after Divine Services by Elder W. Drummond and J. G. Kendrick. First: Delegated Brethren J. J. Gwin, G. Harland and I. P. Murphy to the Bethel Association and as alternates J. C. Bobo and W. J. Sparks and appointed Bro. Bobo to prepare the letter to that body. Second: Received a request, from the Union Church asking for the Eldership of this church to aid her in ordination of a Deacon. The church sent Brethren W. J. Sparks, George Harland, and J. C. Bobo. Then a motion to adjourned was carried. J. C. Bobo, C. C. W. Drummond, Mod.

August 26, 1865. In conference met. After Divine services by Elder Warren Drummond. First: Received and adopted the association letter. Second:

MINUTES OF LOWER FAIRFOREST BAPTIST CHURCH

Agreed to send one dollar for to print the minutes of the Association. J. C. Bobo, C. C. W. Drummond, Mod.

September 1865. No conference.

October 21, 1865. In conference met. After Divine services by Elder Drummond. First: Elected Brother J. J. Erwin Church clerk. Second: Called Elder Drummond to be our pastor for the next year, viz: 1866. J. J. Gwin, C. C. Adjourned. W. Drummond.

November 25, 1865. In conference met. Divine Services by Elder W. Drummond. No business transacted. J. J. Gwin, C. C. W. Drummond, Mod.

December 23, 24 1865. No conference nor preaching on account of troublesome condition of our political affairs that now distract our country. J. J. Gwin, C. C.

January 1866. Saturday 27 No conference, Sunday the 28 Divine services by Bro. W. Drummond. J. J. Gwin, C. C.

February 24, 1866. No conference. Sunday no preaching on account of the nonattendance of our pastor. J.J. Gwin, C. C.

Saturday March 24, 1866. No conference, Sunday 25, 1866 no preaching on account of the nonattendance of our pastor. J. J. Gwin, C. C.

April 21, 1866. Saturday. After Divine Services by Elder W. Drummond received Elder John Gibbs by letter dismissed from New Prospect Church said church having ordained him to preach the Gospel. Sunday the 22 Divine Services by Elder J. Gibbs and W. Drummond. J. J. Gwin, C. C. W. Drummond, Mod.

May 2, 1866. Saturday After the divine services by Elder W. Drummond the church in conference met opened the doors of the church for the reception of members when sister Nancy Lawson came forward and was cordially received. Second: Granted letters of dismission to sisters Ann Barnett and Emily Barnett. Third: Appointed Bro. J.J. Gwin committee of one to wait on Sister Sarah Ann Barnett to inquire of her concerning her misconduct and to report to next conference. Sunday the 27th Divine Services by Bro. Drummond. J. J. Gwin, C. C. W. Drumond, Mod.

June 23, 1866. In conference met. After Divine Services by Elder Drummond the record of the last conference leaving been read, Brother J. J. Gwin the committee of one appointed to wait on Sister Sarah Ann Barnett for the purpose of inquiring of her concerning her past misconduct the committee made his report that he had not been to see her, but had saw Brother B. Sparks he had informed him that the report was true. Adultry being the

68

charge--the committee believing he had done his duty reporting accordingly the church refused to receive the report. Laid the matter on the table.

June 24, 1866. Baptism administered to all candidates at 8 o'clock divine services by Elders W. Drumond and W. F. Lee the church agreed to protract the next regular monthly meeting. J. J. Gwin, C. C. W. Drummond, Mod.

July 21, 1866. Divine Services by Elders J. Gibbs and Drummond elected Brethren J. J. Gwin, G. Harlin and W. Sparks, delegates to represent the church in the association. C. Gibbs in case of failure. Directed the clerk to prepare the association letter, postponed our communion until our August meeting.

July 22, 1866. Sunday. Prayer meeting at 10 o'clock. Preaching by Brethern W. Lee, W. Drummond, J. Gibbs to a large and attentive congregation. We hope great good will be the result.

July 23, 1866. Monday. Prayer meeting at 10 o'clock. Divine services by Elders J. Gibbs, W. Lee, W. Drummond.

July 24, 1866. Tuesday Prayer meeting at 10 o'clock preaching by Brethren W. Drummond, W. Lee and J. Gibbs. The meeting closed with strong manifestations of interest and of a breaking out of a revival among us. J. J. Gwin, C. C. W. Drumond, Mod.

August 25, 1866. In conference met. Saturday our pastor being absent Brother W. Sparks was called to the chare. First: Read and adopted the associational letter, Sunday 26.

September 4, 1866. No conference J. J. Gwin, C. C.

October 27, 1866. In conference met. Granted a letter of dismission to Bro. J. J. Gwin. W. Sparks, Mod.

[No minutes from October 1866 to April 1867]

April 7th 1867. At a called meeting of Lower Fairforest Baptist Church of Christ. 1st: In conference met. Appointed Brother John Gibbs clerk. 2nd: Dismissed Sister Sarah C. Gibbs by letter. Third: Also Elen Williams by letter. 4th: Took up the request of C. Gibbs and upon his request excluded him. 5: A committee of two appointed to labor with Sister Sarah Barnett, J. Gibbs and Wm. Sparks. J. Gibbs, C. C. Morehead, Mod.

April 27, 1867. In conference met. Finding no business except Blank report of committee in the case of sister Sarah Barnett the case was continued to our next. J. Gibbs, C. C. Morehead, Mod.

May, 1867. No meeting

June, 1867 No meeting

July 29 1867. After Divine Services by Br. Brown and Morehead on Sunday evening- the first. First: Dismissed Sister Susan Barnett by letter. Second: Elected George Harlin and Bryan Sparks as delegates to the Bethel Association and I. P. Murphy and William Sparks in case of failure. Third: Appointed Brother J. Gibbs to write the church letter.

August, 1867. No meeting church letter adopted in private by the male members in private consel for the association.

September, 1867. In conference met and after Divine services by Morehead excluded Sister Sarah Barnett for basterdy. Morehead, Mod. J. Gibbs, C.C.

October 1867. No meeting on the account of the rain.

November 23, 1867. In conference met, and after Divine Services by Gibbs and Morehead proceeded to business. First: Restored sister Mary Willard. Second: Granted Sister Mary Willard a letter of dismission. Third: Granted a letter of dismission to Sister Amy Willard. Morehead, Mod. Gibbs, C. C.

December 28, 1867. After Divine Services by G. W. Morehead and Gibbs church met in conference and elected unanimously Br. William Brown to supply us next year and clerk to notify him by letter of said call.
Morehead, Mod. Gibbs, C. C.

[No minutes from January 1868 - March 1868]

April 21st 1868. At or in regular conference after Divine Services the following resolutions were posed viz. Resolve whereas that in the providence of God or in the results of this war now closed we are virtually and nationally and spiritually or religiously be separated from the colored race, therefore, be it resolved that we the Baptist Church of Christ at Lower Fairforest do this day and forever separate ourselves from the Freedman in a religious point of view and authorize our deacons to grant all cordially members of our body of Freedman letters of dismission to join other churches of like faith and order in support the foregoing we say for our justification that the Freedman was virtually declared a nonfellowship with us as they have not been at meeting in about two years and in justification of our selves and for the purpose of Union and harmony we by this act do declare an unfellowship with all the Freedman of our body that does not take letters of dismission accordingly to the foregoing resolutions this done and signed in order and in behalf of the church day and date above. Written and that the foregoing be recorded on the church book. Gibbs, C. C.   Brown., Mod.

May 23, 1868. After divine services by Br. Brown in conference met. First: Received a statement by Br. Brown concerning his ordination from Lower Dunkin Creek Church and upon said statement the church taken up the case and after, some consideration agreed to act in accordance with the suggestions of said church to ordain Br. Brown at this (Lower Fairforest) at our next regular meeting in June and invite Brethren Robertson, Lee, Carter, Dr. Reid, and Pope. Gibbs, C. C.   Brown, Mod.

June 27, 1868. Saturday. After Divine Services by Brown and Gibbs opened the door for the reception of members. Received none. First: Received a communication from Lower Dunkin Creek Church informing us that our request had been granted with regard to the transfer of Br. William Brown's ordination and concluded to ordain him tomorrow at 11 o'clock. Gibbs, C. C. Brown, Mod.

Minutes of Council

An ecclesiastical council called by the Lower Fairforest Church convened at Lower Fairforest this 28 day of June at 11 o'clock Organized by choosing Elder Y. H. Pope moderator and requested Brother Jasper Gibbs to act as clerk. The records of the church relating to the call of this council was read stating the object to the ordination of William Brown. The following churches were represented by the following brethren.

Churches	delegates
New Prospect	Elder Y. H. Pope
Union	Thomas Duckett
Padgette's Creek	Jesse Sparks
	T. W. Williams
	R. M. Robinson

In addition to the above the pastor Elder J. Gibbs and deacon William Sparks of Lower Fairforest with the above included the entire council. The council being formed and approved unanimously by the council. The presbytery then proceeded to the ordination of the candidate in the following manner: Elder Y. H. Pope to preach the ordination sermon. Text: Philippians 2 chapter the latter clause of the 16 verse; ordination prayer by Elder J. Gibbs and charge by the same and hand of fellowship by the council. Presentation of the Bible by Elders Y. H. Pope. Benediction by the candidate. Council desolved. Y. H. Pope, Mod.   Jasper Gibbs, C. C.

August 29, 1868. Saturday. After preaching by Br. Brown, In conference met. First: received Willis Tucker by experience.   Second: Delegated to the association the following brethren: George Harlin, William Sparks, Bryan Sparks and as alternates I. P. Murphy. Appointed the clerk to write the letter to the association and agreed to send $1.50 for minutes.

August 30, 1868. Sunday Preaching in the forenoon and afternoon by Br. Brown. Received by experience Mrs. F. M. Williams.

August 31, 1868. After preaching by Br. Guin received by experience Miss Amanda Harlin.

September 1, 1868. Tuesday meeting continued and after preaching by I. Guinn and Br. Brown received by experience Miss Florence Adams and Miss Greer. Appointed Br. William Sparks and G. Harlin to collect what they can and give to Br. Brown by the first Monday in favor of compensation for the present years services. Church letter received and adopted.
J. Gibbs, C. C.   Brown, Mod.

September 25, 1868. Thursday Elder William Brown attended and preached. First. Received by experience Mrs. Sarah Robinson

November 9, 1868. Sunday after prayer by the pastor J. Gibbs the church organized for business. Made a call for supply for the next year resulted in the choice again of William Brown unanimously.

August 1869. After a lapse of several months, owing to inclement weather and the absence of Bro. Brown the church met at a call meeting and received by experience Miss Laura Wilbourn and Miss Medora Lawson.

February 26, 1870. Saturday. After many months owing to bad weather and other causes the church met and after Divine Services by Br. J. C. Russell adjourned until Sunday.

February 27, 1870. Sunday eleven o'clock after Divine Services by J. C. Russell church organized and proceeded to business. First: Opened the door of the church--none received. Second: called for letters for membership. Third: Received J. C. Russell and wife Letha as members by letter from Mount Zion church, Chester District, S. C. Fourth: Also received by letter Br. Jiles Kirby from Bethesda, Spartanburg, South Carolina. Fifth: We record the death of Br. Willis Tucker who died in 1869. J.Gibbs., Mod. and Clerk

February, 1870. After elaspse of several years of irregular preceding we have met regular this year.

March, 1870. No business of importance.

April 1870. Nothing of great interest.

May 1870. Elected Giles Kirby a deacon he refused to serve.

June, 1870. Received by letter Samuel Harlin and wife, Mira by letter from Putman.

July 1870. Received by letter William R. Gibson and wife Mary and 4 daughters from Lebanan (namely) Martha, Susan, & Amanda [only three names listed]. He is a regular ordained deacon.

September 4, 1870. I hereby hand over to S. Harlin our church book as badly kept for him to enroll all names of the other members and also he and the committee B. Greer, and W. Williams to record the proceeding of the ten days meeting to close today. John Gibbs, C. C. pro tem

September 4, 1870. Church met and proceeded to business. First: Went into the election of delegates to meet the Bethel Baptist Association which resulted in the election of Bro. Gordon Williams, William Gibson, and S. B. Harlin. Second: We have just passed through a protracted meeting one that was characterized by the able expounding of the gospel. Many souls was made to feel the effects of a blessed gospel the result of the meeting was 12. Received by experience: namely, Columbus Bennett, E. G. Park, Pink Briggs, Benj. Greer, G. Williams, Madella Holcomb, Jane Greer, Bettie Adams, Millie Ann Adams, Mary Sanders, Susan Ogles. The meeting closed.
S. B. Harlin, C. C. J. C. Russell, Mod.

October 22, 1870. Church in conference met and went into business. First-- received and adopted the association letter. Second: Proceeded to the call which resulted unanimously in calling Rev. J. C. Russell as pastor. Done in Conference. S. L. Harlin, C. C. J. C. Russell, Mod.

December 5, 1870. Received Brother Jeff Greer and wife Fannie by letter. Owing to the inclement Weather nothing done.

January 21, 1871. Church met held conference. First: Moved to call which resulted in favor of Rev. J. C. Russell. Second: Brother J. Gibbs asked for a letter of dismission which after some discussion was agreed to lay over until next meeting. Third: moved to adjournment. S. B. Harlin, C. C. J. C. Russell, Mod.

February 1871. Church met in conference. First: asked for the reading of the minutes of last meeting which could not be done as the clerk did not have the minutes with him. Second: the clerk was instructed to bring the minutes of the last and present meeting to read at our next meeting. Third: moved and seconded that the call of Rev. J. C. Russell be considered unanimously carried. Fourth: Went into a call for a pastor into a call in favor of Rev. J. C. Russell. S. B. Harlin, C. C. J. C. Russell, Mod.

March 25, 1871. Conference met and proceeded to business. 1st: Granted letters of dismission to Bro. Gordon Williams and wife Medora and Brother J. Gibbs. 2d: Appointed Bro. B. G. Greer Treasurer in place of Bro. Williams. 3d: Appointed a committee of Brethren, Namely B. G. Greer and B. S. Sparks to visit sister Susan Ogles to ascertain her situation and if in their Judgment she is suffering for the want of sustenance to relieve them at once and the church will compensate them at the next meeting. 4th: Passed the resolution offered by Rev. J. C. Russell which read as follows

Whereas we are fully convinced that in order to certain success in raising necessary support the ministry and church at this place it is highly necessary that there should be some practical system adopted by which this church may be governed, therefore: Resolve 1st: that it is the indispensable duty of every member of the church (male and female) to contribute something according as the Lord has prospered us to the support of him whom we have called as our pastor or may hereafter call as such to preach the gospel of our Lord and Savior Jesus Christ.

Resolve: 2d That the officers of this church be invested with the power and authority to ascertain the pecunary standing of each member of this church and inform them what amounts they ought to give in order there may be equality among us and members among us refusing to give something after leaving been reasoned with. Thereby exclude himself or herself from fellowship of this church.

Resolve: 3d, That in order to meet the temporal wants of our pastor and the poor of our church we do promise to make calculation upon the first day of every week of how much the Lord hath prospered us during the previous week and to lay that sum by in store until the day of our regular meeting, at which time the said sum be given to the Treasurer and upon the Treasurer's report to the church of the amount in his hands then the church will give him instructions as to its distribution unless the members who gave it specified beforehand to what further they wanted their contribution given.

Resolve: 4th, That if any member fails to attend church for three consecutive meetings without provincial excuse thereby makes themselves amenable to the church and it shall be the duty of the members of the church to report such delinquency to the officers of the church, ministers of the gospel in regular charges of other Churches are excepted.

Resolve: 5th, that it is our bound duty to instruct the rising generation and being them up in nurture and admonition of the Lord we believe that Sunday Schools are great nurseries for children and a means of grace. We oblige ourselves to organize and labor to keep up a Sunday School at this church and to encourage the children in the apostolic plan of giving.

Moved to elect two deacons at our next meeting. Moved to adjourn. S. B. Harlin, C. C.
J. C. Russell, Mod.

April 24, 1871. Church met and nothing done.

May 22, 1871. In conference met. Nothing of importance.

June 26, 1871. After divine Services by our pastor church met in a business capacity. First: Sister Lizzie (Harlin) colored applied for a letter of dismission opening to the resolutions passed immediately after the war in regard to their nonattendance. They were all regular excluded. She was living in the county at the time there was a committee appointed namely: Bro. C. Harling, William Sparks, S. B. Harlin to inquire into her standing with whom she had been living. No further business. church adjourned. S. B. Harlin, C. C. J. C. Russell, Mod.

July 24, 1871. Owing to the inclemency of the weather nothing done.

August 27, 1871. conference. The committee appointed to inquire into Sister Lizzie Harlins (col) case not being ready to report was laid over to next meeting. Done in conference. B. Harlin, C. C.   J. C. Russell, Mod.

September 22, 1871. First: The committee to inquire into Sister Elizabeth and Berry Harlin case reported favorably-- The church then unanimously consented for them to have a letter of credit and also instructed the clerk to write them. Second: The church then went into the election of delegates to the association which resulted in the choice of the following Brethren viz: W. B. Gibson, Barrum Sparks, and S. B. Harlin and also the pastor, Bro. J. C. Russell to prepare an associational letter. S. Harlin, C C.   J. C. Russell, Mod.

October 26, 1871. Conference. The church met in a business capacity. First: The association letter was read and adopted. No further business. S. B. Harlin, C. C.   J. C. Russell, Mod.

November 25, 1871. The church met in a business capacity. First: Appointed the following Brethren to a committee to look into the delinquent members: Bro. B. G. Greer, William Gibson, and Barrum Sparks. Conference closed. S. B. Harlin, C. C.   J. C. Russell, Mod.

December 22, 1871. In conference. The committee reported that Sister Mary Gibbs wished the church to bear with her a little longer. The church agreed to do so. Adjourned. S. B. Harlin, C. C.   J. C. Russell, Mod.

January 1872. No conference.

February 1872. On account of no pastor no preaching and no conference. S. B. Harlin, C. C.

March 24, 1872. No preaching and no conference.

April 1872.   After preaching by Bro. Gwin the church met in a business capacity. First: Called Bro. Gwin to the supply the church for this year. Second: Granted letters of dismission to Bro. Russell and wife. Third: Motion to adjourn.   B. G. Greer, C. Protem

May, 1872.   After services by the pastor conference no business of any importance transacted. B. G. Greer, C. Protem.   Gwin, Mod.

June, 1872. Preaching by the pastor, after services conference no business of any importance. S. B. Harlin, C. C.   Gwin, Mod.

August, 1872.   Conference agreed to protract our meeting.   Our pastor laboured faithfully assisted by Brother James Lee. Lasted for several days-no accession, but deep interest manifested. S. B. Harlin, C. C.   Gwin, Mod.

September, 1872. conference, No business of importance. S. B. Harlin, C. C. Gwin, Mod.

October, 1872. Conference. Nothing done. S. B. Harlin, C. C. Gwin, Mod.

November, 1872. Conference-- nothing of interest. S. B. Harlin, C. C. Gwin, Mod.

December, 1872. Conference--nothing done. S. B. Harlin, C. C. Gwin, Mod.

January, 1873. No conference on account of bad weather. S. B. Harlin, C.C. Gwin, Mod.

February, 1873. Conference-nothing of interest. S. B. Harlin, C.C. Gwin, Mod.

March, 1873. Conference. Granted letters of dismission to Brother William Gibson and family also agreed to elect a deacon in his place in our next meeting day. Done in conference.   S. B. Harlin., C. C.   Gwin, Mod.

April, 1873.   Conference met.   Received a letter from Brother Joshua Alexander from Lebanan Church. Done in conference. B. G. Greer, Ck. Protem. Gwin, Mod.

May, 1873. Conference met--no business of Importance. S. B. Harlin., C. C. Gwin, Mod.

June, 1873. Conference met-nothing done. S. B. Harlin, C. C.   Gwin, Mod.

July, 1873. Conference met. Appointed a committee to look into the church and see what repairs was needed and also to attend to the work. The committee consisted of the following Brethren: I.P. Murphy, B. Sparks, S. B. Harlin, B. G. Greer and Robert Greer, and Sanford Wilburn added to Committee Conference adjourned. S. B. Harlin, C. C.   Gwin, Mod.

August, 1873. Conference met. Received Bro. Benjamin Greer by experience. Second: Proceeded to the election of delegates to the Bethel Association resulted in the choice of Bro. B. G. Greer, Barrum Sparks, S. B. Harlan. I. P. Murphy, Alternate. Third: Received and adopted the associational letter. S. B. Harlan, C. C.   Gwin, Mod.

MINUTES OF LOWER FAIRFOREST BAPTIST CHURCH

September 1873. No conference.

October 1873. Conference met. First: received Brother James Calhoun Humphries and sisters Alene Margaret Humphries and Louise Josephine Sanders by letters from Hebron Church. Adjourned. S. B. Harlin, C. C. Gwin, Mod.

November, 1873. No conference.

December, 1873. Church in conference. Called Brother Gwin to supply us. S. B. Harlan, C. C. Gwin, Mod.

January, 1874. No conference.

February, 1874. Ascertains that Bro. Gwine cannot preach for us.

1874. Nothing done.

April, 1874. Church meets. Appoints a committee of three Brethren to try to get some one to preach. The committee consisted of Brethern Barrum Sparks, S. B. Harlin, and William Sparks.

May, 1874. Nothing done.

June, 1874. Nothing done.

July, 1874. The committee to get a minister reports of after addressing several ministers that they have not been able to secure the service of one.

August, 1874. In church conference. Elected delegates to the association. Brethern Geo. Harlin, and I. P. Murphy, and William Sparks, S. B. Harlin, Alternate. The clerk to write the associational letter. The church also send - $2.45 for minutes.

September 1874. The association meets with us today and we have secured the services of Bro. F. C. Jeter for the balance of the year.

October, 1874. Preaching by Bro. F. C. Jeter. No business.
S. B. Harlin, C. C. Jeter, Mod.

November 1874. No conference.

December, 1874. Nothing done.

January, 1875. Called Bro. F. C. Jeter.

February 1875. Nothing done

March 1875. No business of any importance.

April 1875. Church in conference. Called Bro. Geo. S. Anderson to supply the balance of the year. Gibbs, Mod.

May 1875. No conference.

June 1875. Exercises by Bro. Gibbs called Bro. C. T. Scaife to commence 2nd Sabbath and in August and Saturday before.

July 1875. Nothing done.

August 1875. Church in conference. Sister Mattie Greer and Elizabeth Greer presented letters from the New Bethel Church and were received into fellowship. The pastor in behalf of the church extended the hand of fellowship. The church then went into an election for delegates which resulted in the choice of Brethren G. Kirby, B. Sparks, and S. B. Harlin, Alternates James Bennett. S. B. Harlin, C. C. C. T. Scaife, Mod.

September 1875. After several days of meeting and the church feeling very much revived and also the good news of the salvations were reechoed in our walls by the humble and contrite who came forward and related what Christ had done for them, made us take courage feeling that the Good Lord must surely be here. There was seventeen who came forward and were received into the church by experience. Namely: A. Judson Gibbs, Gilmer Greer, F. B. Alexander, H. G. Bailey, Jasper Wilburn, Margaret Wilburn, Victoria Wilburn, Florence Sparks, Alice Sparks, Amanda Barnett, Cornelia Barnett, Julia Holcomb, Emma Adams, Henrietta Adams, Pauline Bailey, Medora Bailey, Emma Greer.

At the close of the meeting the church went into conference and a motion prevailing that Brethren Judson Gibbs, Gilmer Greer, and Jasper Wilburn be added to the names of the delegates to the association. The clerk read the associational letter and the same was adopted. Adjourned S. B. Harlin, C. C. Scaife, Mod.

MINUTES OF LOWER FAIRFOREST BAPTIST CHURCH

List of members of Lower Fairforest Church

Males

Robert White
Phillip Holcomb, d. March 7th 1820
Jesse Boatman   d. 1833
Jesse Holcomb
Paton Simmons
James W. Cooper
William White d. Dec'm 6th 1829
Joseph Reeder
Caleb Greer d. Oct. 4th 1834
Joshua Greer
James Boatman
Robert White, Jr.
Joseph Little Dismissed by Letter
Absolom Walker
W. Thomas Willard, Excluded
Benj. Holcomb, dismissed and restored
Daniel Tucker, Excluded
Bennett Tucker, Ex. and returned back
Robert B. Hines, Ex.
Isaac P. Murphy
Thomas Cooper
George Benton   Ex. Restored Ex.
John Mayfield
Battle Mayfield
Charles Thurber Res. Excluded July 21, 1832
P. Woodson Ex. Res.
John Murrell
John Powell
Thomas Hart, d. 1832
Rial Briant
James Harlan
Daniel Jackson
William Bogain
Nevil Holcomb, d. Nov. 7, 1832
Jas. White, Capt.
John Anderson
Elijah Greer d. 1832

--an[?] Harlin
William Gregory
Thurston Coggins d. 1832
Samuel White d. 1832
George Kershaw d. 1832
Mitchel Sparks

John Gibbs
John P. Woodson
James Woodson
Robert Woodson
James Woodson son of Robert
Elias White
Churchhill Gibbs
Thomas Woodson
Avry Little
Clemmon Howard
James Hay
Robert Browning d. 1834
Jason Greer
Monroe Robertson
John Tate
James Roberts
Robert Boatman

Females

Sarah Greer, Sr. d. Jan 14, 1817
Sarah Holcomb
Susanna Semmons
Sarah Greer, Jr. d. Feb. 5, 1823
Rachel Greer
Mary Reeder
Sarah Malone Dead Oct. 1812
Elizabeth Duncan
Elizabeth Cooper
Mary Ann Gregory
Polly Greer
Polly White Rhodes
Sally Jackson Holcomb
Elizabeth Little
Charlotte Murphy
Betsy White
Susanna Whitelock
Diana Boatman d. June 12, 1816
Susanna Walker
Sarah Boatman
Letty Torrance
Elizabeth White, Sr.
Isabel Tucker
Clary Little
Polly Mayfield
Joanna Mayfield
Polly Howard
Sally Boatman .

Polly White
Miriam Cooper
Catherine Bruton
Franky Holcomb
Nancy Holcomb Bennett
Cassy Woodson Perkins
Edith Jackson Murphy
Polly Jackson Harris
Betsy Holcomb Malone
Polly Mulkey Mayfield
Nancy Nix Jackson
Polly Tucker
Susanna Mulkey Holcomb d. 1834
Betty Farmer, d. December 15, 1827
Lavina Greer

Polly Gregory
Nancy Woodson
Sarah Roundtree, d. May 13, 18--
Sarah Steen
Jemimah Lee
Lucinda Lee
Priscilla Gibbs Robertson
Nancy Browning
Betty Bogan
Hannah Greer
Elizabeth Whitlock d. Oct. 1824
Sandel [?] Jackson
Jeney Briant
Elizabeth Briant
Susan White
Susannah Anderson
Milly Jackson, d. Feb. 19, 1830
Harriet Murrell
Jane Coggins
Sarah White
Elizabeth Kershaw
Milly Sparks   d. 1833
Mary Robertson
Mary Carroll
Martha Greer
Holly Sparks
Nancy Murrell
Sarah Greer
Russia White
Nelly Gibbs
Anna White
Priscilla Browning

Sally White widow
Sally White
Nancy Woodson wife of James [Woodson]
Sarah Gibbs
Anna Greer Carroll
Nancy Gregory
Polly Hay
Susan Woodson
Julia Harlan
Polly Tucker
Susan Greer
Dicey Holcomb
Susan Gibbs

A List of Female Members, July 4, 1832.

Sarah Holcombe
Rachel Greer
Mary Reeder
Clary Little
Elizabeth Duncan
Mary Howard D. Jan'y 1839
Sarah Boatman
Elizabeth Hart
Mary Gregory
Nancy Woodson
Sarah Holcomb
Priscialla Robinson
Harriet Murrell Fincher
Elizabeth Kershaw
Margaret Fincher Robinson
Mary Carroll   d. Oct. 1838
Martha Y. Greer d. July 27, 1839
Holly Sparks ex. 1844
Sarah M. Greer D. 1838
Anna White
Priscilla Browning, d. 1840
Sarah White, Senr.
Sarah White, Junr. D. 1845 Augt
Sarah Gibbs
Ann Carroll
Nancy Gregory (John)
Polly Hay
Susan Woodson
Julia Harlin
Polly Tucker Ex. July 24, 1835
Susan R. Greer
Dicey Holcomb

Susan Gibbs   d. 1846
Elizabeth Woodson
Elizabeth Woodson, Sr.
Charlotte Harlin
Anne Anderson
Isabella Tucker   d. 1847
Dicey Sanders
Frances Davis
Eleanor Bishop
Sarah Tate
Betsy Ann Bobo
Polly Greer
Patsy Howard, d. August 1838
Deliah Boatman
Sinia Jackson
Telitha Presley
Elizabeth Sparks
Nancy Aribella Greer
Polly Estes, d. 1850
Lydia Kitchens
Mary Gibbs (Widow)
Jane Rogers
Susan Holcomb
Sarah Stone
Elizabeth Garrett
Elizabeth Murphy
Lucinda Robinson, d. 1840
Nancy Greer
Luera Humphries
Mary Willard
Susan Clark
Nancy Sparks
Elizabeth Sparks
Dicey Holcomb
Nancy Murphy
Nancy Murphy
Charlotte Murphy
Sylvia Murphy
Martha Ann Hodges
Mariah Black
Margaret Bailey
Mary Dukes
Margaret Dukes

List of the Male Members July 4, 1834

Jesse Holcomb d. Sept. 1837
Caleb Greer d. Oct. 1834

Isaac P. Murphy
John Murrell d. 1842
William Gregory d. 1842
George Kershaw
Mitchell Sparks d. July 15, 1836
John Gibbs
John P. Woodson
Robert Woodson
James Woodson
Elias White
Churchhill Gibbs
Thomas Woodson
Clemons Howard
Avry Little d. 1834
James Hay
Aaron Harlin Ex. Aug 23, 1834
Jason Greer d. April 20, 1860
Munroe Robinson
John Tate
Robert Boatman
Benjamin Holcomb
L. C. Thurber
Spencer Greer
James C. Kitchens   ex. July 23, 1836
Jesse Greer
Henry Garrett
Hyram Murphy
William Pressley
Joshua Wilburn ex. in 1846
Joshua Greer d. Oct. 13, 1843
Thomas Hart
David Holcomb
Samuel Harlin

1847 A List of Male Members

Isaac Murphy
John Gibbs
Churchhill Gibbs
James Hay
Jason Greer d. April 21, 1860
Robert Boatman
Hiram B. Murphy
Thomas Hart
David Holccmb
Bird Murphy
Wiley Murphy
Jephta Murphy

Harrison Bailey
John C. Bobo
Sherwood Dukes
John L. Norman
William B. Murphy
John Hay
James Greer
George Harlin
Jesse Sparks
Otha Wilbanks
Jeremiah Bobo
Manley Bobo
C. C. Vaughan
J. L. Bobo
George W. Nance
B. F. Rogers
John Sparks d. at Richmond, Nov. 22, 1862
John C. Bobo
B. F. Rogers
Nevil Holcomb
Byram Sparks
James W. Jones
William T. Sparks
Elder W. F. Lee
William Willard
J. J. Gwin
Elder John Gibbs

Female Members 1847 (White)

Sarah Boatman D. D. Dec'r 1847
Elizabeth Hart
Sarah Gibbs
Polly Hay
Deliliah Boatman
Tebitha Pressley
Nancy A. Carroll D 1848
Mary Sparks
Lidia Kitchens D. Augt 1848
Jane Rogers
Elizabeth Murphy
Nancy Greer D. D June 2nd 1856
Lueza Humphries
Susan Clark
Nancy Bobo Sparks
Elizabeth Wilburn
Dicey Holcomb
Nancy Murphy

Charlotte Murphy Died
Sylvia Murphy
Martha Ann Hodge
Susan Murphy
Mariah Black
Margaret Bailey
Margaret Dukes
Eleanor Comer
Susan A. Deliah Beaty
Sarah Norman
Nancy Bobo
Susan Sparks, Ex.
Nancy White D. Sept 1852
Jane Howard
Julia Murphy
Susan Murphy
Malissa Harland
Susan Smith D. 1850
Milly Sanders
Margaret Beaty
Parry Lawson
Caroline Sparks
Rebecca Bobo
Mary Bobo
Parmelia C. Bobo
Amy Goles D. 1849
Margaret Vaughan
Nancy P. Bobo
Eleanor Tucker
Mary Gibbs
Sarah M. Greer
Elizabeth Robinson. Dd. July 20th 1860.
Rody Burrel
Telitha Lawson
Mary Sparks. Dd. May 1st 1862.
Julia Lawson
Milly White
Dicey Hay
Mary Gibbs Jun.
Nancy Lawson
Mary Jane Greer
Unity Lawson
Peggy Lawson
Lucinda Tucker
Betsey Lawson
Elizabeth Sparks
Jane Sanders
Sarah Holcomb

MINUTES OF LOWER FAIRFOREST BAPTIST CHURCH

Jane Greer
Susan Sparks
Nancy McCreight
Elizabeth Robinson
Sarah Ann Barnet
Nancy Greer
Malissa Lee
Anna[?] Willard
Martha Sanders
Ann Parker
Emily Barnett
Amanda Roberson
Lucinda Tucker
Amanda Sparks
Martha Sparks

Females

Mrs. Mary Gibbs
B. Sparks
Amanda Bearden
Malissa E. Harlin
Holly Sparks
Margaret Bailey
Elizabeth Wilburn
Jane Greer
Elender Tucker
Letha Lawson
Unity Lawson
Lucy Tucker
Jane Greer
Amanda Goodwin
Nancy L. Fincher
Nancy Greer
Matha Bennett
Elmira Harlin
Mary Gibson
Madora Kirby
Eletha Russell
Laura Williams
Medora Williams
S. F. Greer
Peggy Lawson
Nancy Alexander
Mrs. Bailey
Lou Humphries
E. Lawson
Susan Ogles

M. A. Adams
Amanda Harlin
Martha Gibson
Susan Gibson
Sarah Gibson
Amanda Gibson
Florence Adams
Bettie Adams
Mary Adams
Madella Holcomb
Sylvia Murphy
S. B. Greer
Frances Greer
Nancy Nix
Mary A. Wilburn
Victoria Wilburn
Florence Sparks
Alice Sparks
E. C. Barnett
Amanda Barnett
Julia S. Holcomb
Emma T. Adams
Henrietta C. Adams
S. Pauline Bailey
L. Madora Bailey
Emma Greer
Mattie Greer
Elizabeth Greer

Male

[this list apparently duplicated below]

I. P. Murphy
B. Sparks
Rev. J. Gibbs
W. J. Sparks
Geo. Harlan
Saml B. Harlin
Wm Gibson
Rev. J. C. Russell
Gordon Williams
Pink Briggs
Ben G. Greer
Ernest G. Park
Giles Kirby
James Bennett
Jefferson Greer

Isac P. Murphy
B. Sparks
Rev. J. Gibbs
W. J. Sparks
Geo. Harlan
Saml B. Harlin
Wm Gibson
Rev. J. C. Russell
Gordon Williams
Pink Briggs
Ben G. Greer
Ernest G. Park
Giles Kirby
James Bennett
Jefferson Greer
A. Judson Gibbs
Gilmer C. Greer
H. G. Bailey
T[?]. R. Alexander
Jasper Wilborn

Benjamin Greer
Joshua Alexander
James Calhoun Humphries

Blacks, July 4, 1834

Greer) Tony
Hay) Prince
McBeth) Tom
McBeth) George
McBeth) Sally
McBeth) Peter
McBeth) Boson
McBeth) Cudjoe
Rountree) Lewis
McBeth) Paul
McBeth) Nancy
Greer) Clary
Hunt) Phebe
Means) Anthony
Clowney) Agnes
Grimkee) William
Goodwin) Tilda
Palmer) Nelly
Murrell) Jenny
Murphy) Jennie

Murphy) Beck
Duncan) Mima
Mitchel) Deal
Duncan) Delphy
Ison) Mingo D. 1835
Gregory) Jenny
Greer) Sally
McBeth) Jacob
McBeth) Mariah
Askew) Siller
Rice) Barbery
Mitchel) Mariah
Mitchel) Mary d. 1842
Holcombe) Sam
Rice) Dave
Fincher) Primas
Rice) Lawson
McBeth) Celia
McBeth) Margaret
Askew) Nathan
Greer) Dicey Ex. June 27, 1835
Greer) Willis
Reader) Bob gone without a Letter 18--
Murphy) Sally   D. March 185-
Holcombe) Tony D. D. 1838
Holcombe) Jenny
Noland) Charles
Noland) Lucy
Rice) Tiller
Gist) Adam
Murphy) Fanny
Holcomb) Polly
Holcomb) Milly
Harlin) Lizza
Harlin) Nancy
Prewit) Prince Ex. 1835 Res.
Murphy) Jim Ex. 1852
Wilburn) Enoch
Wallace) Sam
Sparks) Jeffrey
Bates) Charles
(Duncan) Delph
(Palmer) Abram
(Crenshaw) Henry
(Wilborn) Jes
(Holcombe) Ben
(Rice) Mima
(Gist) Caty

(Fincher) Mariah
(Beaty) Dinah
(Gibbs) Prince
(McBeth) Bill
(Nolin) Eliza

(Gist) Alsey
(Bogan) Polly
(Nolin) Julia Ex. 1849
(Rice) Edmond
(Jones) George
(Murphy) Eliza
(Prince) Dicey
(Murphy) Fincher
(Nolin) Adam
(Rice) Mary
(Murphy) Julia
(Thompson) Antony
(Harlin) Berry
(Murphy) Caroline
(Rice) Ralph
(Gist) Wyat
(Gist) Adam
(Gibbs) Charles
(Noland) Judy
(Noland) Maria
(McBeth) Rachel
(Murphy) Jim
(Whitmire) Jess
(Gibbs) Hannah
(MacBeth) Kazia
(McBeth) Lucy
(Noland) Tom
(Norris) Bill
(Gee) Judy
(McBeth) Independence
(McBeth) Carolina
(Keenan) Africa   Killed Nov. 10[?], 1865
    "   Nancy
    "   George
Noland Lucy

Ester (Jackson)
Jupiter) Rice
Susan   )
Billy McBeth
Sealy   )
Margaret) McBeth

Polly McBeth
Meser (Murrell)
his wife Jane
Nathan (Ascue)
Annas (McBeth)
Mitchell (Woodson)
Dicey (Belongs to Caleb Greer)
Willis (Thos. Greer)
Bob (Reeders)
Sally (Bird Murphy)
Tony and wife Jenny (Mrs. Dicey Holcomb)
Charles and Lucy (Mr. Noland)

Blacks disbanded from the Roll of this Church for non attendance. Regularly excluded.

March 2, 1834.

Blacks [no date]

Tom Holcomb Dd. April 8th, 1827
Luke Bailey Ex.
Joe Gibbs Dd. July 21st 1832
Sam Greer
Tony Greer
Beck Simmons
Jane Goodwin
Affe Holcomb[?] July 1822 Dd.
Jane (Tom's wife)
Negro Tom Goodwin
Free Negro Judah Dd. Febr 1816
Peggy Hol. Dd.
Delph Isom Gone
Anne Ison Gone
Doll Jackson Dd. 1833
Gibbs Anne
McBeth Prince
Tom
George
Sally
Peter
Boson
Cudjoe
Shadrack Benson Dd. Nov. 5, 1813
Lucy McBeth D. Feb. 16, 1827
Charles Hay Ex.
Nance McBeth
Caty McBeth

Hercules) McBeth [these two names marked through]
Jane   )
Cuffy Little
Phoebe (Hunt)
Betty (Luke) Dd. 1832

Frank & Judah Thomson
Jimmy (J. Thompson)
Anthony (Mrs. Means)
Prince McBeth
George
Tom
Sally
Boron
Peter
Cudjoe
Ann
Ison
Doll
Johnson
Gibbs Anne
Peggy Hol.
Delilah Holcombe
Free negro Judah
Agnes (Clowney)
William (Grimky)
Paul (Thompson)
Fil (Goodwin)
Nellie (Palmer)
Matilda (White)
Frank (White)
Jimmy (Murrel)
Charles (Bates)
Beck (Murphy)
Mima (Duncan)
Deal (J. Mitchel)
Delph (Duncan)
Mingo (Isom)
Lucy (Putman)
Mima (Rice)
Jane (Gregory)
Edith (Harlan)
Sarah (Greer)
Nancy (Thompson)
Barbary (Rice)
Henry (Robinson)
Charles (Bates)
George (Claybrook)

Patsy (Bruton)
Lizzie (Harland)
Cato (Gregory)
Mariah (Mitchell)
Mary (Mitchell)
George (Parham)
Prince (Bates)
Shook (Murphey)
Sam (Holcombe)
Dave (Rice)
Harriet (Gage)
Prince (White)
Lawson (White)
Elbert[?] (McBeth)

A list of Male Members 1876

Robert B. Alexander Dismissed by letter Nov. 25th 1877
Joshua Alexander
Fincher Alexander
Green B. Bailey
Charles M. Bailey
Oliver Barnette
Gilmer C. Greer
George Harlan
Samuel B. Harlan
Calhoun Humphries
Giles Kirby Dismissed by letter March 1877
Isaac Murphy
Earnest Park
William Sparks Died Feb. 11th 1877
Byram Sparks
Jasper Wilburn
James Wilburn
Joseph Sanders
James Bennette

The following received during a revival in August 1877.

William Bailey
E. Bearden
Jesse Holcombe
Jesse Lawson
Wylie Humphries
James Austell
James M. Greer
Wm. Nix

Jerry Bobo
Monroe Bobo Dismissed by letter August ---

The following received on Wednesday after the 4th Sunday in Sept. 1877
Solomon Bobo by Experience
Robert Fincher by Letter
Bird Holcomb by Letter

Female members 1876

Mrs. Nancy Alexander
Miss Margery Alexander
Mrs. Emily A. Adams Dismissed by letter
Miss Florence Adams   "
Miss Bettie Adams   "
Miss Antonio Adams   "
Miss Emma Adams   "
Miss Henrietta Adams   "
Mrs. Margaret Bailey
Mrs. Sallie Bailey
Mrs. Lena Bailey
Miss Paulina Bailey
Miss Laura M. Bailey
Miss Penelope Bailey
Mrs. Martha Barnette
Miss Cornelia Barnette
Miss Amanda Barnette
Miss Lafara Barnette
Mrs. Amanda Bearden
Mrs. Nancy Fincher
Mrs. Jane Greer
Mrs. Mary Jane Greer
Mrs. Nancy Greer
Mrs. Amanda Goodwin
Miss Lizzie Greer
Miss Mattie C. Greer
Miss Emma Greer
Mrs. Mary Gibbs
Miss Addie Gibbs
Mrs. Malissa Harlan
Mrs. Elmira Harlan
Miss Madella Holcomb
Miss Julia Holcomb
Mrs. Louisa Humphries
Mrs. Medora Kirby Dimissed by letter March 1877
Mrs. Unity Lawson Dead
Mrs. Letha Lawson Died 1876

95

Mrs. Peggy Lawson
Mrs. Nancy Nix
Mrs. Elizabeth Sparks
Miss Alice Sparks
Miss Florence Sparks
Miss Octavia Sparks
Mrs. Josephine Sanders
Mrs. Elizabeth Wilburn
Mrs. Laura Williams
Miss Amanda Wilburn
Miss Victoria Wilburn

The following received during a revival in August 1877

Mrs. Elizabeth Mitchell by letter
Miss Sarah A. Spillers   "
Mrs. Mary Holcombe on experience
Mrs. Mary Lawson
Miss Nannie Austell
Mrs. Mary Barnette

The following received on Wednesday after the 4th Sunday in September 1877.

Mrs. Mattie Bobo by experience
Mrs. Medora Holcomb By letter
Miss Alice Briggs   by experience
Miss Mary Lawson   "

List of Male Members 1878.

Joshua Alexander
Fincher Alexander   dismissed by Letter Nov 28
Green Bailey
Charlie M. Bailey
Wm. Bailey
Solomon Bobo
Jerry Bobo
Oliver Barnette
James Austell
Gilmer C. Greer
James M. Greer
E. Bearden
George Harlan
Samuel B. Harlan
Calhoun Humphries
Wylie Humphries
Jesse Holcomb

Bird Holcomb
Robert Fincher
Jesse Lawson
I. P. Murphy
Earnest Park
Wm. Nix
Byram Sparks
Jasper Wilburn
James Wilburn
James Bennette
Joseph Sanders

Recd by experience during a revival in July. Baptized in August
Hicks Barnette
Wm. Mitchel
Walton Sparks
J. C. Bobo recd by letter

List of Female Members 1878.

Mrs. Nancy Alexander
Miss Margery Alexander Dismissed by letter Nov 23rd
Mrs. Sallie Bailey
Mrs. Peggy Bailey
Mrs. Lena Bailey
Miss Lena Bailey
Miss Laura Bailey
Miss Pennie Bailey
Miss Penelope Bailey
Mrs. Mary Barnette
Miss Fair Barnette
Miss Ann Barnette
Miss Cornelia Barnette Died Sept. 2nd 1878
Mrs. Martha Barnette
Mrs. Amanda Bearden
Mrs. Nancy Fincher
Mrs. Jane Greer
Mrs. M. Jane Greer
Mrs. Nancy Greer
Mrs. Amanda Goodin
Mrs. Mary Gibbs
Miss Addie Gibbs
Miss Lizzie Greer
Miss Mattie Greer
Miss Emma Greer
Mrs. Malissa Harlan
Mrs. Elmira Harlan
Mrs. Mary Holcomb

Miss Madella Holcomb
Miss Julia Holcomb
Mrs. Louisa Humphries
Mrs. Nannie (Austel) Humphries Dismissed by letter
Mrs. Peggy Lawson Died Feb 22nd 1879
Mrs. Nancy Nix
Mrs. Elizabeth Sparks
Miss Alice Sparks
Miss Florence Sparks
Miss Octavia Sparks
Mrs. Josephine Sanders
Miss Sarah A. Spillers
Miss Mary Lawson
Mrs. Mary Lawson
Mrs. Elizabeth Mitchell
Mrs. Alice (Briggs) Prince

Mrs. Elizabeth Wilburn
Mrs. Laura Williams Dismissed by letter Sept. 27, 1889
Miss Mandie Wilburn
Miss Victoria Wilburn
Mrs. Martha Bobo
Mrs. Holly Sparks died
Mrs. Amanda (Harlan) Smith

Recd by experience in July during a revival. Baptized in August
Miss Polly Bailey
Miss Kate young
Mrs. Sallie (Clifton) Bobo dismissed by letter Jany 27th 1880
Miss Julia Bobo
Miss Sallie Mitchel[?]
Miss Carrie Harlan
Miss Mary Barnette
Miss Artie Bennette
Mrs. Nancy Bobo recd by letter
Miss Sallie Bobo recd by letter

List of members 1880.

Joshua Alexander   Died
Nancy Alexander
Green Bailey
Lena Bailey
Wm Bailey
Sallie Bailey
Polly Bailey
Lina Bailey
Laura Bailey

Charlie Bailey
Pennie Bailey
Solomon Bobo
Martha Bobo
J. C. Bobo received by letter Nov. 23rd 1878
Nancy Bobo
Jerry Bobo
Sallie Bobo received by letter
Julia Bobo
Mary Barnette
Oliver Barnette
Fair Barnette
Ann Barnette
E. Bearden
Amanda Bearden
Gilmer Greer
Lizzie Greer
Jane Greer
S. Jane Greer
James Greer Excluded Aug 1881
Mary Gibbs
Addie Gibbs
Louisa Humphries
Wylie Humphries dismissed by letter May 27, 1882
Calhoun Humphries excluded
Jesse Holcomb
Mary Holcomb
Adella Holcomb
Julia Holcomb
Bird Holcomb
Madora Holcomb
Robert Fincher
Nancy Fincher
Jesse Lawson
Mary Lawson
Byram Sparks
Elizabeth Sparks
Alice (Sparks) Greer
Florence Sparks Nix died Nov. 1880
Octa Sparks dismissed by letter Feby 27 --
Walton Sparks
I. P. Murphy
Margaret Bailey
Mary Lawson
Elizabeth Wilbourne
Amanda Wilbourne Ray dismissed letter --
James Wilbourne
Victoria Wilbourne

Jasper Wilbourne
Mattie (Greer) Wilbourne
James Bennette
Artie Bennette
Joseph Sanders
Josephine Sanders
Nancy Greer
Hick Barnette
Wm. Mitchel
Amanda Barnette
Mary Barnette
Elizabeth Mitchel
Sallie Mitchel
Sarah (Spillers) Danniel
Alice (Briggs) Prince
Nancy Nix
Wm Nix
Holly Sparks   died Aug --
Kate Young
Carrie Harlan   dismissed June 1890[?]
Martha Barnette
Amanda Goodin
Amanda (Harlan) Smith dismissed Sept 188-
W. C. Harrison   recd by letter July 188-
Fannie Wilbourne   "
Emeline Lawson   "
Mary Lawson   " March
Sarah A. Barnett   died Aug 1882
Benjamin Greer

1884

Nancy Alexander
Green Bailey
Lena Bailey
Wm Bailey
Sallie Bailey
Polly Bailey
Laura Bailey
Charlie Bailey
Pennie Bailey
Solomon Bobo
Martha Bobo
J. C. Bobo
Nancy Bobo   died 1887
Jery Bobo   dismissed by letter 1886
Sallie (Bobo) Lawson

Julia Bobo
Mary Barnette
Fair Barnette
Oliver Barnette
Ann Barnette
Eliphes Bearden
Amanda Bearden
Gilmer Greer
Lizzie Greer
Jane Greer died Jany 1887
S. Jane Greer
Mary Gibbs died 1891
Addie Gibbes diss. by letter
Louisa Humphries
Jesse Holcomb died 1885
Mary Holcomb
Adella Holcomb
Bird Holcomb
Madora Holcomb
Robert Fincher
Nancy Fincher
Jesse Lawson
Mary Lawson
Byram Sparks
Elizabeth Sparks
Walter Sparks
Emma Sparks
Esther Sparks
I. P. Murphy died July 2nd 1886
Margaret Bailey
Mary (Bobo) Lawson
John Gilbert
Mary Gilbert
Elizabeth Wilbourne died Feb 1885
Vic Wilbourne
James Wilbourne
Jasper Wilbourne
Mattie (Greer) Wilbourne
James Bennette
Artie Bennette
Joseph Sanders
Josephene Sanders
Nancy Greer died March 11, 1885
Hix Barnette
Amanda (Barnette) Bailey
Elizabeth Mitchel dead
Sallie Mitchel
Alice (Bride Prince) dismissed by letter

Nancy Nix
Wm Nix
Julia Nix
Kate (Young) Alverson dismissed
Martha Barnette
W. C. Harrison
Emeline Lawson
Fannie Wilbourne
Mary (Bobo) Lawson
Earnest Park
Alice (Sparks) Greer
Amanda Goodwin
Benjamin Greer died April 1884
Octavia Sparks Willis dismissed by letter Aug 24th
Louisa Barnette recd by exp. Sept. 84
Bery Lawson
Jasper Lawson died
William Edmonds
Rebecca Edwards
Robert Wilbourn
John Fincher
Mrs. Fincher
Howard Williams
Will Edwards
Carrie Barnette
Alice Bailey
Minnie Bobo
Walter Greer
Aletha Holcomb
Lena Holcomb
Robert McBeth died
Giles Greer
Louisa Greer

1891

Y. S. Bobo died 1902
Martha Bobo died 1911
Nannie Bobo
Eliphus Bearden Died
Amanda Bearden Died
Annie Bearden Died
J. C. Bobo Died
Wm. Bailey Died
Sallie Bailey Died
Polly Bailey
Laura Bailey Died
Lena Bailey

Pennie Bailey
Green Bailey Dis
Lena Bailey Dis
Mary Barnette Died
Fair Barnette
Ann Barnette
Oliver Barnette
Carrie Barnette Excluded
Miranda Barnette
Martha Barnette
Blanch (Barnette) McDaniel Dismissed
Nannie (Barnette) Betanbeaugh
Charlie Bailey
Alice Bailey
Wm. Edwards
Rebecca Edwards
Will Edwards
Robert Fincher
Nancy Fincher
John Fincher
Mrs. John Fincher
James Bennette
Amanda Goodwin
John Gilbert
Mary Gilbert
Gilmer Greer
Lizzie Greer
Giles Greer
Louisa Greer
Jane Greer
Alice Greer
Mattie Greer Bishop
W. C. Harrison
Mary Holcombe died
Adella Holcomb dismissed
Bird Holcomb died
Jesse Lawson
Mary Lawson
Bery Lawson
Mary Lawson
Elizabeth Mitchel
Sallie Mitchel
Byram Sparks
Elizabeth Sparks
Emma Sparks
Walter Sparks
Esther Sparks
Lula Sparks

Lizzie Sparks
Joseph Sanders
Josephene Sanders
Gus Sanders
Lou Sanders
Mat Sanders
Hicks Barnette   died
Robert McBeth   died
Mary Gibbs died
Jasper Wilbourne
Mattie Wilbourne
James Wilbourne
Robert Wilbourne
Nancy Nix   Died July 25, 1906
Wm Nix
Julia Nix   dead
Fannie Wilbourne
Howard Williams
Sarah (Spillers) McDaniel
Nancy Alexander
Mrs. James Bennette
Lucy McDanniel
Lawrence Bishop
Kate Lawson
Jesse Lawson
James Eubanks
Cornelia Eubanks
J. W. Sweat
Daisy Humphries[?]
Nannie Sanders
Charner Lawson   Dead
John Lawson   Dead

List of Church Members 1906

Eliphus Bearden
Gilmer C. Greer
S. A. Elizabeth Greer
Gilmer G. Blankenship
Mason A. Blankenship
Wm C. Nix
Alice (Greer) Nix   Died Sept. 12th 1911
Bennie Greer
Emma (Lawson) Greer
Walter Greer
Nancy Nix died July 25, 1906
Norman Nix
Charles Bailey

Alice Bailey
Polly Bailey
Lina Bailey   died Sept 28, 1906
Pennie Bailey
Walter Sparks
Emma Sparks
W. Perry Duckett
Esther (Sparks) Duckett
Lawrence G. Bishop
Lula (Sparks) Bishop
Lizzie (Sparks) Estes
Oliver R. Barnett
Lafara Barnette
Ann Barnette
Miranda Barnette
Margaret Barnette
Hicks Barnette died Feb. 5, 1911
Martha A. Bobo died Feb. 17, 1911
Joseph A. Smith
Nannie Bobo Smith
Robert Smith died 1906
Nettie (Williams) Smith
Rosa (Smith) Vinson
Horry Barnett
Charley Lawson
Lettie (Humphries) Lawson
Jesse Lawson
Carrie (Davis) Lawson
Mary Lawson
Kate Lawson
Robert Lawson
Monroe Lawson
Berry Lawson
Jasper Wilburn
Mattie (Greer) Wilburn
Emma Wilburn
Manly Wilburn
Scaife Wilburn
Eloise Wilburn
Mrs. Fannie Wilburn
Miss Fannie Wilburn
Bessie Wilburn
Emma (Wilburn) Gist
Robert Fincher
Nancy Fincher
John Fincher & wife
Jesse Lawson died
Bird Holcomb died June 12, 1910

Sallie Mitchel
Jane Greer died Dec. 9th 1908
Sallie (Greer) Bishop
Margaret (Bishop) Grainger dismissed by letter Feb. 1st, 1914
Mattie (Greer) Bishop
Nancy Alexander
Blanch (Barnett) McDaniel
Grace Wilburn
Lee Wilburn
Ben Wilburn
Robert Bailey
Robert Greer
Eloise Greer
Vera Bishop
Florence Duckett
Robert Barnett
Furman Wilburn
Gordon Bishop
Annie Wilburn
Mary Bishop
Victoria Greer
J. M. Bond
Mary Meador Wilburn
George G. Bishop
Sue Greer
Hattie Vinson dismissed July 21st, 1914
C. A. Granger dismissed by letter Feb. 1st, 1914
Earl Bishop
Emma Lee Duckett
Bessie Greer
Jemima Wilburn granted letter 9/4/25
Monroe Gregory
Adella Gregory
Judson F. Bishop
Mrs. J. F. Bishop
Fant Bishop
Mrs. Hassie Barnett
Charles Bishop
Beno Mitchel
Eugene Greer
Bennie Bishop
Lillian Bishop
Mary Rice
B. F. Rodgers

INDEX

Prepared by James D. McKain

(BOBO) Solomon 95, 96, 99, 100
  Spencer 26
  W. W. 63
  Y. S. 102
BOGAIN, William 79
BOGAN 41
  Betty 81
  Polly (Black) 41, 91
BOND, J. M. 106
BOOKER, J. 22
BORON, (Black) 92, 93
BOSON, (Negro) 4
BREWTON, Catharine 15
  George 15
  Patsy 15
Brick Meeting House 1
BRIDE, Alice (Prince) 101
BRIGGS, Alice 96
  Alice (Prince) 98, 100
  Pink 73, 88, 89
BROWN, 70
  William 70-72
BROWNING, Nancy 17, 81
  Priscilla 16, 30, 81, 82
  Robert 17, 80
BRUTON, Catherine 8, 81
  George 8-11
  Patsy (Black) 94
BRYANT/BRIANT 32
  Elizabeth 81
  Jeney 81
  Philip (Negro) 32
  Rial 79
BULLINGTON, Dicey 9
  Robt. 2
BULLINTON, Nancy 11
BURMAH 24
BURREL, Rody 86
Cane Creek 38
Cap[?]. Charles (Negro) 4
CARROLL, Ann 82
  Anna Greer 82
  Mary 16,81,82
  Nancy A. 85
CARTER, 71
  G. 66
  I. G. 63
  J. C. 62,65,67
  J. G. 62-67
CATO, (Negro) 13
Charles (Negro) 4

CHARLES, Hayes 8
CHEAK 41, 45
CHURCH
  Brushy Fork 37
  Calvery 59
  Catawba 38
  Cavalry 60
  Congaree 63
  Cool Branch 53, 54
  Corrinth 59
  Fairforest 2, 7, 18
  Flat Creek, Hall County Georgia 19
  Hebron 77
  Hopewell 37
  Lebanan 76
  Liberty 59
  Lower Dunkin Creek 70, 71
  Lower Fairforest 1, 48, 69-71
  Mount Zion, Chester District, S. C., 72
  New Bethel 78
  New Hope 2, 32, 36, 37
  New Prospect 44, 59, 63, 64, 68, 71
  Pacolet 63
  Padgett's Creek 1, 2, 4, 17, 18, 25, 26, 31, 33, 34, 63, 71
  Philadelphia 59
  Sharon Baptist, Henry County Georgia 17
  Tinker Creek 3,4
  Union 28, 59, 64, 67, 71
  Unity 62
  Upper Fairforest 4, 17, 18, 25, 26, 29, 47
  Woodward Baptist 18
CLARK, Susan 32, 83, 85
CLAYBROOK, George (Black) 93
CLIFTON, Sallie (Bobo) 98
CLOWNEY 27
  Agnes (Black) 9, 27, 89, 93
COGGINS, Jane 81
  Johnson 14
  Thurston 79
COMER, Eleanor 39, 54, 86
COOPER, Elizabeth 5, 80
  J. W. 5
  James 1
  James W. 2, 3, 79

(COOPER) Miriam 8,81
　Thomas 8-10, 12, 79
CRENSHAW, Henry (Black) 90
CUDJOE (Black) 92, 93
CUFFY (Negro) 3, 4, 6, 8
DANNIEL, Sarah (Spillers) 100
DAVID/DAVITT, Ben (Negro) 9
　William 9
DAVIS, Carrie (Lawson) 105
　Frances 19, 23, 83
　J. 18
DELPHY (Colored) 51, 59, 60
DEMANS, W. 44
DOLL (Black) 3, 93
DOLPH (Negro) 3
DRUMMOND, S. 55
　W. 68, 69
　Warren 67
DUCKETT, Emma Lee 106
　Esther (Sparks) 105
　Florence 106
　Thomas 71
　W. Perry 105
DUKES, Margaret 43, 83, 86
　Mary 43, 83
　Sherwood 41, 43, 85
DUNCAN, 11, 21, 33, 35
　C. 26
　Charlotte 40
　D. 31, 34, 36-39
　Delf (Negro) 11
　Delph/y (Black) 90,93
　Elizabeth 80, 82
　Jessy (Negro) 21
　Mary Howard 82
　Mima (Black) 90,93
　Minna (Negro) 11
EDMONDS, William 102
EDWARDS, Rebecca 102, 103
　William 102, 103
ELLIS, Mary 58, 60
ENOCH (Negro) 26, 38
ERWIN, J. J. 68
ESTES, Lizzie (Sparks) 105
　Polly 21, 45, 83
EUBANKS, Cornelia 104
　James 104
EZELL 50
FANT, 44
　E. 39
FARMER, Betty 10, 81

FELDER, 44, 50
　C. 53
FINCHER, 22, 102
　Harriet 29
　Harriet Murrell 82
　John 102, 103, 105
　Mariah (Black) 22, 91
　Mary 29
　Nancy 95, 97, 99, 101, 103, 105
　Nancy L. 87
　Primas (Black) 90
　Robert 95, 97, 99, 101, 103, 105
FRANK 14
　(Negro) 9
GAGE 47
　Harriet (Black) 47,94
GARRETT, Elizabeth 23, 24, 83
　Henry 23, 24, 84
GEE 55
　Judy (Black) 55,91
GEORGE (Black) 92, 93
GEORGIA, Gwinnett County 23
　Hall County 19
　Henry County 17
GIBBS 3, 43, 49, 78
　A. Judson 78, 98
　Addie 95, 97, 99, 101
　C. 28, 32, 36, 50, 52, 54, 55, 58,
　　60-65, 69
　Charles (Black) 47, 91
　Churchhill 17, 29, 59, 64, 80, 84
　Ellen 62
　Hannah (Black) 52, 91
　J. 18, 22, 28, 30, 36, 38, 40-46, 48,
　　51, 53, 57, 59-61, 63, 64, 69-73,
　　88, 89
　Jane 44, 55
　Jasper 71
　Joe 16
　Joe (Black) 92
　John 16, 18, 21, 23, 24, 26, 27,
　　29, 31-34, 37, 45, 47, 50, 52, 54,
　　56, 58, 59, 68, 69, 73, 80, 84, 85
　Judson 78
　Laura 64
　Mary 21-23, 41, 52, 75, 83, 86, 87,
　　95, 97, 99, 101, 104
　Nellie (Norman) 18
　Nelly 16, 81
　Prince (Black) 91
　Priscilla 10

(MURRELL) John 10, 33, 79, 84
  Meser (Black) 92
  Nancy 81
NANCE, George 47
  George W. 44, 85
NEWLIN 44
NIX, Alice (Greer) 104
  Ben. 2
  Florence Sparks 99
  Julia 102, 104
  Nancy 9, 88, 96, 98, 100, 102, 104
  Norman 104
  Wm. 94, 97, 100, 102, 104
  Wm. C. 104
NOLAND 43, 49, 55, 57, 66, 67
  Adam (Colored) 43, 66, 67
  Charles (Black) 90, 92
  Judy (Black) 49, 91
  Lucy (Black) 90-92
  Marie/a (Black) 49, 91
  Tom (Black) 55, 57, 66, 67, 91
NOLIN 40, 43
  Adam (Black) 91
  Eliza (Black) 35, 36, 91
  G. S. 35
  J. Nix (Negro) 40
  Julia (Black) 40, 43, 44, 91
NOLON 49
  Adams (Negro) 49
NORMAN, C. C. 48
  J. 42
  J. L. 43-49
  John L. 50, 85
  Nelly (Gibbs) 18
  Sarah 41, 86
NORRIS 55, 57
  Bill (Black) 55, 91
  Judy (Colored) 57
OGLES, Amy 42, 43
  Susan 73, 87
OLD ABRAM (Negro) 56
OWINGS 44
  C. C. 46, 47
  M. C. 40-42, 44-46, 48
PALMER 21, 29, 30
  Abram (Black) 21, 30, 90, 94
  Daniel 9
  Lotty 55
  Nelly/ie (Black) 9, 89, 93
PARHAM, George (Black) 94
PARK, E. G. 73

Earnest 94, 97, 102
  Ernest G. 88, 89
PARKER, Ann 87
PARKS, Ann 63
PARSLEY, C. C. 47
PATSY, Howard 21
PEG (Negro) 2
PERKINS, Cassey 14
  Cassy Woodson 81
PETER (Black) 4, 92, 93
PHILLIPS, G. W. 63
PICKET, G. W. 59
PINES, B. B. 14
POPE, 71
  Y. H. 71
POWEL/L, John 10, 11, 79
PRESLEY/PRESSLEY 32, 34, 35
  Letitha 32
  T. K. 50
  Tebitha 85
  Teletha 21, 83
  William 29, 31, 34, 84
PREWIT 19
  Prince (Black) 19, 90
PRINCE (Colored) 8, 20, 47
  42, 56
  Alice (Bride) 101
  Alice (Briggs) 98, 100
  Dicey (Black) 42, 56, 91
  Jenny (Colored) 56
  McBeth 4
  McBeth (Black) 92
  Sam (Colored) 56
  William 57
  Willis (Colored) 56
PRUETTE, Cipryan 59
PRUITT, Ann 65
PURSELEY, William 24
PUTMAN 72
  Lucy (Black) 93
PUTMEN, Lucy 15
RAY, A. 24, 35
  Amanda Wilbourne 99
  James 26
  T. 24, 26, 28, 30, 31
  Thomas 1
READER/REEDER 17
  Bob (Black) 17, 90, 92
  Joseph 7, 9, 79
  Mary 4, 80, 82
REID 71

(WHITE) Benj. 33
  Betsy 80
  E. 22, 26, 27, 31, 33
  Elias 16, 18, 20, 23-25, 39, 80, 84
  Elizabeth 3, 13, 15, 80
  Frank (Black) 10, 93
  I. 60
  J. 59
  J. C. 59
  Jas. 79
  John 10, 18, 32
  Julius 56, 58
  Lawson (Black) 94
  Matilda (Black) 10, 93
  Milly 42, 86
  Nancy 17, 42, 86
  Polly 7, 9, 81
  Prince (Black) 94
  Robert 2, 5, 9, 13, 79
  Russia 16, 81
  Russia (Wilbanks) 18
  Sally 16, 82
  Samuel 14, 15, 79
  Sarah 14, 15, 38, 81, 82
  Susan 81
  W. 2
  William 1, 2, 5-10, 12, 13, 79
WHITLOCK 7
  Elizabeth 81
  Susanna 1, 3, 8, 80
  Thomas 2
WHITMIRE 52, 53
  Jesse (Black) 52, 53, 91
WHYAT, (Colored) 38
WILBANKS, Otha 85 (see also
    Willbanks)
  Russia (White) 18
WILBORN 21, 38
  J. 34
  James (Negro) 21
  Jasper 89
  Jesse (Negro) 38, 90
  Joshua 30,39
WILBOURN/E (see also Wilburn)
  Elizabeth 99, 101
  Fannie 100, 102, 104
  James 99, 101, 104
  Jasper 100, 101, 104
  Laura 72
  Mattie 104
  Mattie (Greer) 100, 101

  Robert 102, 104
  Vic 101
  Victoria 99
WILBURN 34 (see also
    Wilbourne)
  Amanda 96
  Annie 106
  Ben 106
  Bessie 105
  Elizabeth 85, 87, 96, 98
  Eloise 105
  Emma 105
  Emma (Gist) 105
  Enoch (Black) 21, 90
  Fannie 105
  Furman 106
  Grace 106
  James 94, 97
  Jasper 78, 94, 97, 105
  Jemima 106
  Joshua 84
  Lee 106
  Mandie 98
  Manly 105
  Margaret 78
  Mary A. 88
  Mary Meador 106
  Mattie (Greer) 105
  Sanford 76
  Scaife 105
  Victoria 78, 88, 96, 98
WILLARD, Amy 70
  Anna 62, 87
  Mary 32, 70, 83
  Polly 20, 21, 38
  Thomas 13, 15
  W. Thomas 79
  William 62, 65, 66, 85
WILLBANKS, Otha 42, 43
WILLIAMS, Elen 69
  F. M. 71
  G. 73
  Gordon 73, 88, 89
  Howard 102, 104
  Laura 87, 96, 98
  Medora 73, 87
  Nettie (Smith) 105
  T. W. 71
  Ulyses 64
  W. 73
WILLIARD 66

Herritage Books by Brent H. Holcomb:

*Ancestors and Descendants of Charles Humphries (d. 1837)
of Union District, South Carolina, 1677–1984*

Bute County, North Carolina, Land Grant Plats and Land Entries

*CD: Early Records of Fishing Creek Presbyterian Church,
Chester County, South Carolina, 1799–1859*

CD: Kershaw County, South Carolina, Minutes of the County Court, 1791–1799

CD: Marriage and Death Notices from The Charleston [S.C.] Observer, *1827–1845*

CD: South Carolina, Volume 1

*CD: Winton (Barnwell) County, South Carolina Minutes of
County Court and Will Book 1, 1785–1791*

*Chester County, South Carolina, Deed Abstracts,
Volume I: 1785–1799 [1768–1799] Deed Book A-F*

Chester County, South Carolina, Will Abstracts: 1787–1838 [1776–1838]

Death and Marriage Notices from the Watchman *and* Observer, *1845–1855*

*Early Records of Fishing Creek Presbyterian Church, Chester County,
South Carolina, 1799–1859, with Appendices of the Visitation List of
Rev. John Simpson, 1774–1776 and the Cemetery Roster, 1762–1979*
Brent H. Holcomb and Elmer O. Parker

Guide to South Carolina Genealogical Research and Records, Revised

Jackson of North Pacolet: Descendants of Samuel Jackson, Sr.

Kershaw County, South Carolina, Minutes of the County Court, 1791–1799

Laurens County, South Carolina, Minutes of the County Court, 1786–1789

*Lower Fairforest Baptist Church, Union County, South Carolina:
Minutes 1809–1875, Membership Lists through 1906*

*Marriage and Death Notices from Columbia, South Carolina Newspapers, 1838–1860;
Including Legal Notices from Burnt Counties*

Marriage and Death Notices from Baptist Newspapers of South Carolina, 1835–1865

Marriage and Death Notices from The Charleston Observer, *1827–1845*

Marriage and Death Notices from the
Charleston, South Carolina, Mercury, *1822–1832*

Marriage and Death Notices from the Southern Presbyterian:
*Volume I: 1847–1865
Volume II: 1865–1879
Volume III: 1880–1891
Volume IV: 1892–1908*

*Marriage and Death Notices from the Up-Country of South Carolina
as Taken from Greenville Newspapers, 1826–1863*

Memorialized Records of Lexington District, South Carolina, 1814–1825

*Newberry County, South Carolina Deed Abstracts,
Volume I: Deed Books A-B, 1785–1794 [1751–1794]*

*Newberry County, South Carolina Deed Abstracts,
Volume II: Deed Books C, D-2, and D, 1794–1800 [1765–1800]*

www.ingramcontent.com/pod-product-compliance
Lightning Source LLC
Chambersburg PA
CBHW072159270326
41930CB00011B/2487